JOURNEY TO AFRICA

DEDICATION

This book is dedicated to Don L. Lee, one of the shapers of the Black Tomorrow, without whose persistence and persuasion the book would not exist. (July, 1971)

Journey to Africa

by

HOYT W. FULLER

WTP
THIRD
WORLD
PRESS
Chicago, Illinois

First Edition
Second Printing 1991

Copyright © 1971 by Hoyt W. Fuller

Library of Congress Catalogue No. 72-171224

For permission to reproduce any part of this book in any form,
write to Third World Press, 7524 S. Cottage Grove Ave, Chicago, IL 60619

"The African Actuality: A Personal Journey"
first appeared in the Journal of Black Poetry.

Manufactured in the United States of America
Cover design and illustration by Cassandra Malone.

CONTENTS

SÉKOU TOURÉ
A NEW KIND OF LEADER   7

A JOURNEY TO AFRICA   17

THE AFRICAN ACTUALITY:
A PERSONAL JOURNEY   71

"... Thus the white European mind has worked, and worked the more feverishly because Africa is the Land of the Twentieth Century...."

—W. E. B. Du Bois

"... Political power today is but the weapon to force economic power. Tomorrow, it may give us spiritual vision and artistic sensibility. Today, it gives us or tries to give us bread and butter, and those classes or nations or races who are without it starve, and starvation is the weapon of the white world to reduce them to slavery...."

—W. E. B. Du Bois

January 1959
Conakry, Guinea

SÉKOU TOURÉ

A New Kind of Leader

THE RECEPTION ROOM, SMALL AND UNASSUMING for a presidential palace, was also sticky hot. Somewhere behind a divan the motor of an air-conditioning unit whirred without wafting a breeze or dispelling the thickening odor of human sweat.

Across from me, the prim, dacron-suited emissary from the Israeli Embassy at Accra wiggled and gasped, flashing a miserable smile in a futile effort to disguise his utter misery. The sun-browned, shirt-sleeved Frenchmen in the room watched him squirm with malicious delight. They were old hands at the discomforts of Africa. They could take it.

Around the room, a waiting African occasionally glanced at the diplomat, sometimes with sympathy, sometimes with suspicion. A lean African in dandy-bright black and white shoes leaned forward and spoke. "Why don't you take your coat off?" he asked in French.

The diplomat knew only a few words of French and did not understand. He smiled dumbly at the African and appealed to me. I told him what the African had suggested. It was unthinkable. "No, I have an appointment at four o'clock with President Touré," he explained. "It's nearly four now."

But at four o'clock one of the uniformed palace guards who act as pages stepped in and read another name from a reception slip. A muscular young African in shorts jumped up and bounded to the door, following the guard into the verandah and up the stairs to the president's suite.

The diplomat frowned and, in an elaborate gesture that punctuated his outrage, raised his arm and regarded his watch.

Before the guard finally came in and read the diplomat's name more than a half hour later, two other Africans had been summoned from the room to interviews with their president. They had been waiting longer.

While the diplomat—perhaps not unduly—was raw with fury and probably gravely humiliated, no slight was intended. The incident served to point up some of the crippling inadequacies besetting the six month old Republic of Guinea.

The swaddling nation has only one ambassador-at-large (able and youthful Sorbonne graduate Diallo Telli) to receive and entertain visiting diplomats, and he is often representing the country elsewhere. The palace's two English-speaking aides, who could have assisted the diplomat, are usually neck-deep in interpretative work.

Sékou Touré: A New Kind of Leader

The Secretary of State, suave, granite-hard Fodé Cissé, must be as breathlessly busy—if not as widely traveled—as John Foster Dulles at the height of the American's world-girdling pursuit of his controversial foreign policy.

But more than anything else, the spectacle of a foreign diplomat taking his turn in line with ordinary citizens is indicative of the revolutionary personality in Guinea's presidential palace. For, even with adequate facilities and assistance, there remains the possibility that Sékou Touré would have received callers as they came.

In understanding Sékou Touré, it is better to realize at the offset that he is something absolutely new in world leaders and on the African scene. In the first place, at 37, he is perhaps the youngest chief of a non-monarchial member of the United Nations. He is also the only one of Africa's glittering galaxy of black leaders without a formal university education.

And, as president of the French West Africa-wide, 700,-000-strong Union of Black African Workers (Union Generale des Travailleurs de l'Afrique Noire), he is the only national leader in the world who is also chief of a powerful international labor union.

American and European journalists like to compare Touré with Kwame Nkrumah, president of Guinea's sister-nation Ghana a few hundred miles down the Atlantic Coast. But, apart from their color and their mutual aim in asserting the black man's claim to a decisive voice in the destiny of Africa, there are few similarities between them.

Much is made of the legend that Touré is grandson of the mighty Almany Samory Touré, the last of the Malinké warriors who waged valiant but futile war against the French conquerors of Guinea. Touré is noncommittal to the point of evasiveness about this illustrous chapter in his ancestry, but he readily admits the more pedestrian fact that he was born to peasant parents in the village of Faranah in 1922.

He studied at the École Coranique, the Moslem training school, and at primary and technical schools in Kankan and Conakry, the capital. Whatever other academic education he received was absorbed through independent reading and correspondence courses from Paris.

The practical education that catapulted Touré into the arena of politics began with his first important job as a postal and telegraph worker in 1941. He learned about union organizing and the politics of labor, the most bare-knuckled and savage of the breed.

But Sékou Touré is the hard-muscled, iron-nerved type who thrives on the difficult. With characteristic shrewdness and skill, he soon rose to the job of general secretary of the postal and telegraph union. After that, he never stopped rising. When he was voted to the top position in the French West African labor movement last January, he climaxed a steady advance of labor jobs that—in the past 15 years—covered virtually every important labor post in the French West African territories.

The American and European press has also made much of Touré's Marxist orientation. Inevitably, in his rise to power in conjunction with France's then Communist-dominated General Confederation of Labor, he was associated with Communists. He was even courted by them and packed off to a series of conferences in Warsaw and Prague. But, while asserting an adherence to Marxism, Touré denies he is a Communist.

"It seems to have become the custom to say that all governments that modify their economic conditions and the social and cultural systems imposed on them by colonialism are inspired by Marxism," Touré said. "The political unity

Sékou Touré: A New Kind of Leader 11

of Guinea is no more the consequence of Marxism than is the independence of our country.

"It is possible that certain forms of Marxist organization respond best to the particular conditions of underdeveloped countries. It is even possible that certain structures of inspiration derived from Marxist conception respond better than all the others to the given realities of underdeveloped countries which are determined to overcome their enormous backwardness. But this is not the same as putting our people to the service of one philosophy or the other."

Dynamic is a puny word to describe the husky, handsome, hard-driving young head of Africa's newest independent nation, but it is more apt than any other. It is his extraordinary dynamism, cloaking boundless energy and passionate ambition, which enabled him to combine union activities with political interests and to scale both heights simultaneously.

At the same time that Touré was gaining his initial labor leader experience as general secretary of the postal and telegraph union, he was one of the founders of the R.D.A. (Rassemblement Democratique Africain), French Africa's majority party. While climbing uninterruptedly up the labor ladder, he also held practically every important office in Guinea. He became, in turn, chief of the territorial assembly, mayor of Conakry (population 80,000; 5,000 Europeans), and deputy to the French National Assembly at Paris.

By the time he became vice president of the Guinea Council of Government in 1957, Touré had been for five years head of the P.D.G. (Parti Democratique de Guinée), the Guinea arm of the R.D.A., and undisputed political chief of the territory.

When, in September, 1958, Touré told France's De

Gaulle that Guinea preferred "poverty in freedom to riches in slavery," he spoke for the nation. Guineans backed their leader with a staggering 98 percent vote for independence, and Sékou Touré rode into the presidency on a wave of acclamation.

Critics of former colonial countries frequently charge that the new African and Asian leaders play fast and fancy with democratic precepts. Touré dismisses such criticism with sharp, incisive observations.

"Africa is not Europe or America," he says. And to explain what he means, he cites the ancient tribal traditions of Africa which remain strong even among Africans with European or American educations. These traditions are many and varied, but an over-riding characteristic of all African tribes is a deep respect for—and faith in—the established authority.

In the past, particularly in British-occupied Africa, this adherence to tradition was the instrument through which the colonialists ruled. To bring the people under their sway, the colonialists had only to bend the tribal chieftains to their will.

Now, as demonstrated in both Guinea and Ghana, the Africans' age-old custom of following a strong leader is part of the key to the phenomenal popularity and power of the new political chiefs.

Touré's second answer to his critics is this: "They say we are not democratic, but they had the chance to show us what democracy is, and they never did it."

He speaks from bitter experience. In his ascent to power, the French sought to silence him by exiling him to a job in another territory. Touré quit the job and returned to Conakry. He later led the strikes which won the first major pay raises and benefits for French West African workers.

In his cool, cunning manner, Sékou Touré exploits the natural tendency of the 2,500,000 inhabitants to almost deify their leader. By exhorting the population to extra effort in what he terms his "human investment" program, he succeeds in getting them to work long hours in the blistering heat or torrential rain building roads, bridges, clinics and schools.

By convincing the people that they will be performing a patriotic duty, he persuades them to merge land and labor in the experimental communal farming of rice, an important food staple.

To insure overwhelming turnouts at political rallies or to induce the populace of Conakry to clean the littered streets, Touré has only to tape a brief speech and have it broadcasted intermittenly over Radio Guinea (nine hours a day broadcasting time.)

He is a gifted speaker who, with a minimum of words, can transform an audience of enraptured Guineans into an obedient chorus, breathlessly still or deafeningly loud, as he wants it.

He is a grand actor, a dramatic performer of the first rank, and many who have come to sneer have left murmuring grudging praise. He is aloof and imperious or warm and generous as the occasion seems to demand, or he can be all these things within a matter of minutes.

I met Touré first on the sun-parched suburban football field the day delegates to the U.G.T.A.N. elected him president. Dignitaries and guests sat on a natural earth mound in front of 30,000 milling, cheering Guineans, and Touré the people's idol was as serenely regal as an ebony god. His fine brown eyes flashed like a hot, searching flame in my face and he acknowledged our introduction with courtesy but no smile.

Two days later I met him again in his spacious office on the top floor of the three-story white-stone mansion built for French governors. He seemed, misleadingly, half his broad-shouldered, six-feet size behind the great desk. On the wall in back of him hung an enlarged photograph of himself and Nkrumah taken on the occasion of the Ghana-Guinea "union" at Accra last November. On the opposite wall were two giant portraits of Nkrumah and President Tubman of Liberia, who had gifted his new neighboring Head of State with a sleek, sky-blue 1959 De Soto sedan.

Touré did not rise to meet me. He shook hands from behind the desk, studying me with the dagger-sharp, fire-brown eyes. He was cautious, wary, like a man fighting a duel. Only toward the end of the interview did the eyes cease their probing and the strong jaw relax.

The next time I met Touré he came smiling from behind his desk, shook my hand warmly and threw a comradely arm around my shoulder. "And how is my American friend today?" he asked. We stood together at the window and looked through the spreading branches of the dinosaur-like fromager tree across the rolling palace grounds to the sea.

We talked casually of Guinea and of its problems and needs until Touré's secretary rushed in to announce the unexpected arrival of the American consul general from Dakar. Immediately Touré assumed another role. He became the gracious but serious Chief of State, the guarded fencer in the treacherous game of international politics.

Sékou Touré is a man of many moods and parts. And, perhaps, above all, he is a man possessed with a sense of mission. That mission seems to be to lead his people forward into the modern industrial age in the shortest possible time. Beyond that, it is to raise the status of the African so that

Sékou Touré: A New Kind of Leader 15

he stands on equal footing with any other man in any other place.

When I arrived in Conakry there were two imposing statues of former French governors of Guinea in different parts of the city, one of them in the small park (Place Ballay) opposite the presidential palace. One morning, on my way to the palace, I saw a band of workmen tearing down the statues. It was a graphically dramatic symbol of the mood of Touré—and perhaps of all black Africa.

That evening Touré told me that a new history of Guinea would be written for the nation's schools, and that black heroes would replace men like George Poiret and Noel Ballay whom the French had immortalized with bronze monuments.

"They say that we are anti-white or anti-western, but that is not the case," Touré said. "We are simply pro-Africa and pro-African. It certainly is time somebody was."

And it is that attitude which explains why Sékou Touré can let an elegant, educated diplomat cool his heels in a hot, airless room with simple, perhaps illiterate Africans. For a long, long while the African has been made to wait to the last. Now, at last, he can take his turn.

". . . The world regards us (U.S.A.) with amazement: we are leading the 'Free World.' We champion 'Democracy' and for this we stage Little Rock, drive Negroes from the polls, chase black students with bloodhounds, and throttle free speech. On top of this Africa arises and our FBI trains a 'Peace Corps' to guide it. . . ."

—W. E. B. Du Bois, 1958

Febuary 1959

A JOURNEY TO AFRICA

OFTEN DURING MY FIRST YEAR OF VOLUNTARY exile in Europe in 1958, thinking with ambivalent feelings about the inevitable time when I would have to go home again, lines from a poem by the French poet Charles Pierre Baudelaire would haunt me . . .
"You'll not find another place, you'll not find another sea.
This city is going to follow you. You'll stray
In the same streets. In the same suburbs you'll grow gray;
Amid these same houses you'll reach old age.
You'll always find this city. Another?—It's a mirage . . ."
I had run away from America. It was an old, many times told story. In the year before I packed up and sailed to France I had spent much of the time futilely trying to find some slot in which I could fit with a reasonable degree of comfort and satisfaction. I had quit *EBONY* magazine, for the magazine did not seem to be moving in any direction

that it seemed important for me to go, and it was extremely difficult in 1957 to find meaningful work that also would not threaten my sense of racial integrity in the white publishing world. I could adjust neither to what seemed to me irrelevance nor to "tokenism" in employment, and that meant that my alternatives were effectively exhausted. I could not play the game of "making it" when the cost of winning was the loss of my self respect.

My failure to find an acceptable job was not the most important reason for my flight to Europe. It was merely the ultimate spur. Every single day in America had brought moments when there was need to find some refuge from the nerve-wrenching reality of the omnipresent war of race. A report of some incident in the papers, the rudeness of some waiter in a restaurant, a walk through the Black slums or a drive (it had to be a drive) through a white suburb, an encounter with some unwittingly patronizing "liberal"— any of these things, and countless others. But even more than these things, the terrible apathy of "educated" and "affluent" Black people plunged me into impotent rage. Three years after the Supreme Court had ruled school segregation to be unconstitutional, bigots had unleashed a virtual reign of racist terror against Black people all over the country, and the response of the ablest, most articulate and resourceful segment of the Black population was pathetic: they either tucked their tails and said nothing, fearing to risk their jobs or their status; or else they mouthed the same old cliché about "discrimination" and "justice" and "equality" that Black people had been safely echoing for 300 years. In Chicago, where a unified stand of a few hundred influential Blacks would have turned the political machine into panic, the reaction against police brutality and economic colonialism was shameful silence. And Chicago was merely prototypical. Black people seemed to lack the courage to act in their own self-interest. I had seen Europe before, and I knew it was not "another place." Still, in Europe there was at least temporary escape from the poisonous climate of hate and oppression that threatens to smother America.

For more than a year I lived in a salmon-colored miniature villa that sits in the middle of a huge garden off the main street of Terreno, one of the foreign-occupied subdivisions of Palma de Mallorca. It is a lovely, romantic house, surrounded by flowers and fruit trees, and I was happy there. Sometimes as I sat in the living room and gazed out at the people and traffic beyond the garden, the realization would crowd in on me that in no similar resort city in my own country would I be able to live unharassed in such a setting. On these occasions the old rage would stage its abortive riot in me and I would turn for relief to pleasanter thought than home. I found myself thinking more frequently of Africa. I had for years nursed a vague ambition to go there. Why not now?

The decision then—not the desire—was sudden. I knew that, being so close to the African continent as the mid-Mediterranean, I would forever regret it if I did not, whatever the difficulties, make the effort. I also thought that I would—if I liked it and if it was possible—try to find some work there, perhaps tutoring English privately. I thought I would like to spend a year in Africa, if no longer. Perhaps what talents I possessed would be needed. I decided on the new Republic of Guinea for two reasons: first, because I wanted practice in the French language; and second, because the country was now independent and it was not necessary to apply for a visa to France which ordinarily makes certain restrictions on visits by foreigners to its African territories.

When I mentioned to a French friend in Palma that I

was planning a trip to Guinea, he said: "Africa is not what you think. You will be disappointed." This was four months after a muscular, iron-jawed Malinkéan with a legendary ancestry had led the territory to sever its political links with France. In rejecting Charles de Gaulle's crucial new constitution, Sékou Touré had found appropriately dramatic words with which history could record the moment. "We prefer poverty in freedom," he had orated, "to riches in slavery."

My French friend, being understandably patriotic, was unimpressed with Touré's brave rhetoric. "They'll find out there's more to independence than a lot of hot air," he said. "Before a year has passed they'll be crying for the French to come back."

And then he told a Guinea story currently making the rounds among Palma's French nationals. The story went that the day following the fact of independence, a block-long queue had formed outside the Conakry railroad station awaiting the through train to Niger. Guineans who had never been able to afford a train ride flocked to the station. But when told that they would still have to buy tickets, just as before, a roar of disillusioned protest ran through the crowd. "What good is independence," they demanded, "if you can't ride free?"

It was certainly a relevant story. To many subject peoples the word independence is pregnant with a great many idealistic foetuses destined to be still-born. But like so many others who either regret or deride the surge of these peoples toward self-determination, my French friend missed the point. That point is that the subjugated are determined to assert what they believe to be their right to rule themselves. And if, as is likely, being no better nor weaker than other men, they sometimes rule badly, well, it is a family affair.

I did not argue my friend's prediction that I would be

disappointed in Africa nor his presumption as to the purpose of my projected journey, partly, I recognized, because of subterranean uncertainties as to my own motives. I had told myself, and others, that I was going to so-called Black Africa to see for myself what it was like. Undoubtedly there was another reason, a deeper one. Perhaps I felt there was an answer to a crucial question that only actual experience in Africa could give. Perhaps I was about to embark on a compulsive spiritual pilgrimage and perhaps my French friend, wiser and more perceiving than I, understood this and understood also that such nebulous and mystical journeys are prone to disillusion.

In any case, the voyage from Palma to Conakry would take nine days, the ship sailing south to Algiers then past Gibraltar to Casablanca and around the continental bulge to Dakar and Conakry. There would be time to think and things to see, and for the moment I was willing to settle for that.

I had also been warned by my French friend that traveling third class on the Marshal Foch to Guinea would in no way approximate my Atlantic crossing on the Liberté. That both ships were French was about all they had in common. So I was prepared for the worst. The cabin for three to which I was assigned, therefore, came as a pleasant surprise. It was rectangular and roomy, with more than adequate space for three bunks and the luggage and apparel of its trio of occupants.

I was also fortunate in my cabinmates. One was a tall, thin, whitehaired and fiftyish Canadian on a leisurely journey to Johannesburg. Mr. Abraham was landing at Dakar and traveling overland to Nigeria, through the Congo and the Central African Federation. He was a sociable fellow, loved to talk—especially about baseball—and since he knew only a few words of French was very much relieved to have someone to speak English with. Unfortunately I knew nothing of baseball. The cabin's other occupant was a Frenchman, a businessman, he said, short, dark, sturdily built, with a wry sense of humor and an earthily, easy manner. M. Gimet was debarking at Dakar.

It was in the third-class dining room that the difference between the famed French Line and Africa route's Frassinet & Cyprien Fabré was, at first, most noticeable. The room was a squat, cramped quarter with a roof of ivory-painted pipes. Two portholes were windows, and a four-foot counter served as bar and store. Tables were oblong, built for eight, with benches, mess-hall style, and the poor food was served indifferently by a French sailor and a wiry, gray-haired African, both dressed in anything they cared to wear.

There were two dining shifts in third-class. Mine included soldiers in and out of uniform, priests and nuns, several French families, a beaming little African who looked like a pygmy, and a silent, sallow-skinned Arab woman in flannel robes.

M. Gimet was one of the two civilians at my table. The other was a grotesquely disfigured young man with only two perfectly formed fingers on each hand and a face and neck that looked as if they had been severely burned in childhood. The other five people at the table were soldiers. Three were from the French Antilles, the only Blacks in a contingent of soldiers sailing for Abidjan.

One of the Antillians knew a few English words and phrases. M. Gimet spoke Spanish. The others spoke only French. The jabs at America began almost immediately after I was introduced to the table at dinner the first night out. "Is it true," the bearded soldier beside me asked, "that Americans eat hamburgers and salad and ice cream all on the same plate?" This light-headed maliciousness did not let up throughout the voyage. And sometimes the jibes were vicious.

The dining room, between meals, served as third-class lounge but was used primarily by the crew. The larger, more elegant second-class lounge was open to third-class passengers who spent most of their time there and on the surrounding decks. The Foch and a sister-ship, the Jean Mermoz, were used mainly to transport French government personnel and their families, troops and missionaries, and the emphasis was on utility rather than luxury.

After dinner, I walked on the decks with Mr. Abraham. He was a restless, long-legged bachelor, addicted to taking long hikes, and he felt hemmed-in on the ship. As we paced up and down, talking, I battled silently and not very successfully against seasickness. Mr. Abraham said he had only recently retired from a Toronto bank, had sailed to London, flown to Paris, took a train to Marseille where he had boarded the ship the previous day. He planned to make business contacts in Lagos, Salisbury and Pretoria. I soon surrendered to a whirling head and abandoned the promenade but Mr. Abraham went on stalking the decks long after I had gone below.

Algiers loomed in the distance when I mounted to the deck early the next morning. It was a fabulous sight. In the pre-dawn darkness the city lay like a dazzlingly jeweled mound against the sky. It was, of course, illusory. When I came up again after breakfast Algiers in the daylight was no jewel. It was impressive, though. Built on hills, the city rises from the sea and stretches out on both sides so that, from the sea, it looks like a giant octopus in repose. An octopus scourged with cancer. The left side of the giant head is bright and healthy; the right side gutted and ravaged like a diseased cheek.

Passengers needed only their boarding tickets to go ashore. I went in the morning with two Africans, Yao Kouame and Keita Faraban. Yao had been studying in Paris and was going home to the Ivory Coast to take a job in the treasury department at Abidjan. Keita, a 17-year-old, was going home to Guinea from a French technical school at Marseille. We strolled the bustling streets of the modern city, the left side of the octopus's head, and we might have been in a well-heeled section of Paris. We had coffee and *croissants* in a cafe attended by a young Algerian, bought papers and postcards, and then set out for the Casbah. On the way we met M. Gimet. He said he had just been turned away from the Casbah by the *gendarmes*. "They won't let you in," he told us. "There's a police barricade down there."

Yao and Keita thought it best not to try to enter the Casbah under the circumstances, and I reluctantly acceded to their decision. Up to that point we had not mentioned the Algerian war, although I had been thinking about it. I then asked Yao what he thought the outcome would be. "It is difficult to say," he said, "but I hope the Algerians will have their independence." He seemed hesitant to venture beyond that statement. Keita also said he hoped the Algerians would gain independence.

Apart from the attendant in the cafe, most of the Algerians we saw were women, veiled and unveiled, burnoused old men, and young boys. Tension was not apparent, and downtown Algiers seemed a long way from war. That was the impression until Keita pointed to the *Palais de Justice*. Several uniformed French officers loitered in front of the building, and machine guns behind barbed wire pointed out at us. After that we noted the the *prefecture* and other public buildings had guards and similar gun emplacements. Several military installations were rather obtrusive near the Casbah, and soldiers wandered about the area with tommy guns slung over their shoulders.

After lunch aboard ship I returned to the city alone. I did not want to spend an entire day in Algiers without making a serious attempt to get into the Casbah. Without Yao and Keita, I was willing to risk a rebuff. Prior to boarding the Foch I had held the somewhat hazy notion that my being an Afro-American would insure a relatively safe reception in the quarter. Although I knew very well in advance that American-style racial segregation was not a feature of the French Army, it had not occurred to me that Blacks were among the troops being used against the Algerians. The three Antillians in the military unit aboard ship were argument to the contrary. I therefore had no basis for pleading with officials who might try to bar me from the Casbah. As it was, perusasion proved unnecessary. No one tried to stop me.

The Casbah, in all probability, has not changed since millions of motion picture fans were first introduced to it through the movie *Algiers*. But, perhaps not surprisingly, it is a far less entrancing place without Hedy Lamarr and Charles Boyer. There is, undeniably, a certain ancient and Oriental charm in the narrow, steep and winding cobblestone passageways. The Arabs, whether quiet and watchful or roguishly commercial, were for me figures out of an exotic world. But the dark alleys and curves beyond the squares and bazaars are fouled with the overpowering stench of urine, and the astonishing little gardens and patios hidden deep in that adobe maze hardly compensate for the incredible squalor. I did not linger long in that fabled quarter.

When I returned to the ship shortly before the 6 p.m.

sailing deadline, the bow was crammed with African soldiers. They had been relieved of duty after two years in Algeria, and those who were not being mustered out of service were en route to Abidjan. The soldiers looked exceedingly unsoldierly. They wore heavy woolen uniforms that were universally in need of naptha baths, a hodge-podge of unmilitary shoes and shirts and socks. Their appearance contrasted rather sharply with that of the group of soldiers traveling in third class.

I went to the railing of the first-class deck that overlooked the bow and spoke to an intelligent looking soldier standing on the staircase. He smiled and shook hands firmly, as if he really meant it. I was to learn that shaking hands is a custom among Africans. And they do mean it. It is their way of saying "friend." I asked the soldier, a corporal, where he was from, and he said Cotonou. "I'm going home," he said. "I'm all through with the service."

He said he had not actually been in combat against the Algerians but had served in what sounded, from his description, like a quartermaster outfit. There were, he said, African soldiers fighting the Algerians, and many had been killed. But he did not want to talk about Algeria. He had been briefly in Paris and had a brother who was studying thére to be a lawyer. "We used to see American Blacks on the streets, but they would never speak to us," he said. "They always acted as though they didn't see us. Why is that so?"

I could not answer the question.

"Don't they know we are brothers?" he asked. "It is necessary to speak, to shake hands, and be friends."

In the lounge that evening I met Sylvester and Jeanne Whitaker and their eighteen months old son, Mark. Syl, a Princeton graduate and a Black American, had a political science fellowship and was en route to Kano in Northern

A Journey to Africa

Nigeria to observe the political situation and the effects of self-government beginning in that region in March. Jeanne, French-born, was a language professor at Swarthmore, where she and Syl had met as students. They had spent the past six months in London where Syl had met Africans and Africanists, studied Hausa, the language of Northern Nigeria, and received orientation on his project. In France they had visited Jeanne's parents, former missionaries to Madagascar. They would debark at Porto-Novo in Dahomey, since the ship stopped only at French ports, and drive to Kano in their Land Rover in the ship's hold.

The information had spread that I was going to Guinea and some of the reactions to this news were curious. "Ah, Touré needs help already!" taunted a ship's officer. One of the French soldiers said: "The Americans don't waste much time moving in!" Another implied that Guinea would be annexed to Liberia, "that other American colony." Even some of the Africans seemed to assume I was on some sort of government mission. It was just as well. When I explained that I was going on my own, they took it as granted that I was rich.

In the cabin, in the absence of Mr. Abraham, M. Gimet aired a few opinions of both Americans and Africans. He spoke of Americans he had met in Casablanca and his native Bordeaux, a uniformly unattractive lot, apparently. "Americans are always boasting of what they have," he said. "We have homes and automobiles and refrigerators in France too, you know. But French people don't spend all their money on such things. They put it in the bank."

He said that Guinea had gone to pot now that the French had departed. "They don't know how to do anything. You will find out." He felt the French had as much right in Algeria as the Arabs and that the country would revert to savagery if the French pulled out—which they must never do. "It's like Morocco," he said. "You will see when we get to Casablanca. It used to be a great, prosperous city. But all the businesses are closing down since the Moroccans took over. Now, nothing's doing there. I lived in Casablanca until two years ago. I had to leave."

I asked him why he "had to leave" and why other Frenchmen had left. Did the fact that the government was controlled by Moroccans rather than Frenchmen mean that Frenchmen could not do business there?

"It's not the same," he said. "They don't know what they are doing. Furthermore, Americans have moved into Casablanca in droves since the end of the war. Half the businesses there are owned by Americans."

Upstairs in the lounge I first saw Daniel Guèye, a short, powerfully built Senegalese, the color of hard coal, with a small, round face, beautiful teeth and a perpetual—and deceptive—smile. He wore a brilliant orange-red sweater and trousers as close-fitting as ballet tights. His companion was a lovely red-haired Algerian girl in green velvet lounge pants.

Daniel, garrulous and irrepressible, was always in motion, spatially or vocally. He said he was a chemical engineer in Algiers, that his wife was a Frenchwoman, that his father was mayor of Dakar, his uncle head of the postoffice at Conakry, that he was en route to attend a chemical conference at St. Louis (Senegal), and that he had a Dauphine in the ship's hold, the shipping expense accounting for his traveling third-class rather than first. He spoke English slightly better than the Antillian soldier, but not much better, and had an affection for the word "boy." "My wife is beautiful, boy, truly, more beautiful than this Arab girl, boy. This Arab girl, she white, you know, boy."

A Journey to Africa

Daniel and Odile, the Arab girl, dined on my shift but at another table. All during dinner that night he kept smiling and nodding in my direction. He collared me on my way out his second day aboard. He wanted to tell me he had been to Alabama and Kansas City, accompanying his father on a business trip several years before. In France, he sometimes passed as an American, he said with great pride. There were bars and nightclubs in Toulon and Marseille which wouldn't admit Africans but welcomed American Blacks. "I say, 'I from Alabama, I American boy, not African boy.' I always get in."

He borrowed my Parker ballpoint to scribble some addresses for me, his father's in Dakar, his uncle's in Conakry. All the while he kept noisily ordering beer and drinking and treating anyone who cared to be treated. When I finally decided to go, my ballpoint had vanished. Daniel insisted he had returned it. I knew he had not. I left without my pen.

Mr. Abraham introduced me to an English-speaking soldier at his table who wanted to discuss Little Rock. "There's so much about it in the papers," he said. "Perhaps you will explain me the difficulty." I agreed to meet him on deck the following day. I had known it would happen. I had been "explaining" Little Rock to Europeans ever since I had been in Europe. In Bern, Geneva, Barcelona, Palma. Only in Paris had I been spared questions about the school desegregation problem in America. The Parisians had been preoccupied with a problem of their own: the threat of revolution.

The mysterious looking Arab woman stopped in a passageway to chat. She had been on a visit to her son in Paris. He owned a shop, she said. She liked France but was happy to be back in Africa. She was debarking at Casablanca the following morning. She wished me a good journey.

3

Casablanca, unlike Algiers, does not rise up from the harbor but lies a few minutes away on mostly level land. As its name denotes, it is a white city, while Algiers strikes the eye as gray, and it seems spacious rather than cramped. It is an attractive city and, like Algiers, quite French. The medinahs, the Moroccan versions of the Casbah, are equally teeming and squalid. Many Moroccans are "Black," I was surprised to see. An unusual number of the bus drivers and civil servants might have been refugees from Chicago's South Side. A friendly Frenchman, a merchant who had no plans to quit the city, treated me to a drive through the villa-thick suburbs and along the new white beach where many of the pastel houses and hotels are occupied by American Air Force personnel.

All along the avenue leading from the harbor, and in the heart of town, flashily dressed young hustlers called out, "Hey, man!", and sidled up to peddle anything from watches to women in the latest jive jargon. This breed had been noticeably absent on the streets of downtown Algiers.

M. Gimet was right that many French businesses had closed, and the city lacked the bustling pace of Algiers. I met him in the city and he pressed the point further. "You should go and eat at the *Dragon d'Or*," he said. "Wonderful food. Best Oriental restaurant in Africa. But business is terrible. The patron said he can hardly afford to stay open since the French left." I did not have enough francs for dinner and M. Gimet gladly loaned me 500 until I got back to the ship.

The Moroccan policemen must be among the handsomest in the world. They are assuredly the most courteous and helpful I have ever encountered. When approached, they salute and say, "At your service, monsieur." And though it is obviously a matter of routine, they are so doggoned amiable about it that it seems entirely spontaneous.

Back aboard ship I chatted with Yao while African noncommissioned officers, having somehow spruced up their uniforms or, perhaps, changed them, sang calypso-like tunes to banjo music. Yao, like so many educated Africans I had met in America and in Paris, was extraordinarily well-read, quietly intelligent, with a firm grasp of the economic and political factors at work in the world. He was no ardent admirer of Felix Houphouet-Boigny, the premier of the Ivory Coast and the perennial African member of French cabinets, including De Gaulle's. "Houphouet-Boigny is shrewd, and he is rich," Yao said. "He owns a vast coffee plantation on the outskirts of Abidjan. But I think he no longer speaks for the younger Ivory Coaster."

Later, in Conakry, I learned that Sékou Touré, the 37-year-old president of Guinea, had not abandoned the ambition of wresting leadership of the R.D.A. (Rassemblement Democratique Africain), French Africa's majority party, from Houphouet-Boigny. Marxist-oriented Touré was impatient with the older man's conservatism. Houphouet-Boigny had made no secret of his belief that wealthy Ivory Coast would only suffer by severing the silver cord with France. Touré thought that maintaining the cord is the cause of the impoverishment of Africans in the territories.

Though Yao would not recommend snatching immediate control of the Ivory Coast from the French, his own sympathies seemed to lie more with Touré than with his own premier. He was going home to work and to learn the business of government. He was patient. He felt there was time. A native of a small village deep in the interior, Yao and his wife and young son lived in Treichville, the African quarter of Abidjan. Then, is there segregation in Abidjan?

"Well, not officially," Yao smiled. "Africans can live in the French sector if they can afford it. But only a very few can afford it."

Twice during the day I saw Daniel and deliberately avoided him. That tactic had the desired result. After dinner, Syl Whitaker brought my ballpoint. "Daniel said he had been drinking heavily and didn't remember putting your pen in his pocket," Syl said. It was entirely possible that Syl had exerted influence on Daniel. Certainly he did not hesitate to chide the exuberant African. Once, after a particularly virulent attack by Daniel on the whole white race ("All white people are dogs!" he declared), Syl asked him if he did not think that racism was just as objectionable when Africans practiced it as when whites did. Daniel was not impressed.

Daniel, of course, was a complete fraud. Not only had he stolen my pen, but almost everything he told me turned out to be false. He was not married, neither to a Frenchwoman nor anyone else; his father was not Lamine Guèye, mayor of Dakar, and the address he gave me (I discovered en route back to Europe) was the residence of a French lawyer with the same last name; and the postmaster at Conakry had never heard of Daniel Guèye.

A Frenchman I did not remember seeing before came up and said, "You are American?" I admitted as much. "You are going to Guinea?" I confessed that I was. He nodded, smiled wryly, and walked away. Later, on the deck, I saw him sitting with a group of civilians. As I passed, he ostentatiously bent over and whispered something and all eyes immediately raised to inspect me. Often during the remainder of the voyage I would glance up during a stroll or a conversation and find one or more of this group staring at me with a sort of uneasy sneer.

A Journey to Africa

I kept my rendezvous with M. Jourdan who wanted to talk about Little Rock. We stood on deck and leaned against the railing in the sun. I did not want to be closed away with him in some corner where some passerby could not occasionally interrupt. "It's a terrible thing for America," he said. I tried to keep the thing light, introducing levity I did not feel, but M. Jourdan was determined to favor me with his unwelcome gift of sympathy. The man had several times visited America as a sailor in his youth. He knew New York and Virginia, and he described with a sad shake of his darkly graying head indignities he had seen Blacks endure in Norfolk. "It's a terrible thing," he kept repeating.

4

The morning after Casablanca, bowing to Daniel's persistent entreaties, I went with him to listen to records on his "pick-up." The cabin into which he led me was shared by Odile, the Arab girl, and a tall, thin African girl with whom I had seen Odile on deck. Odile, seasick, lay in the upper berth looking miserable. The African girl, Fanta, was practicing shorthand on the lower berth. She was, she said, a secretary at Dakar, returning from a vacation visit to Algiers. I apologized for breaking in on them and turned to go, but Fanta asked that I stay so that she could test her English. Daniel went to the corner, set up the record player and drew out a case of LP albums, all bearing labels with his name on them. He prefaced the playing of each record with authoritative views of the musicians' ability and status and ruthlessly stopped the machine if a number came up that he did not like. He dismissed Louis Armstrong as "a clown boy." He was fond of Belafonte and Sammy Davis Jr., and had favorites among Cuban and Latin Americans who were unknown to me. He proceeded to interrupt Fanta and me so often that Fanta decided to give up her English lesson.

Daniel was fascinated by the business of color and race in America. The portraits of Belafonte on the albums showed the singer as being rose-tan, and Daniel had difficulty reconciling these pictures with the word "Negro." After several flanking questions, he finally asked point-blank if Belafonte was a Negro, *"un noir."* I said he was. Later, Syl's racial identification seemed to confuse Dainel as much. Syl is what Negro Americans sometimes term "muddy-yellow," and like Belafonte he has stiff, tangled hair. Is M. Syl a Negro too?" Daniel asked with elaborate casualness, as if the answer—whatever it was—would only confirm what he already knew. I said Syl was a Negro. "And his wife?" I explained that Jeanne was white and French. "Ah, she is French!" he exclaimed, nodding his head. Apparently, the fact of her French nationality explained the phenomenon of her union with an American Negro.

Daniel was not the only passenger aboard ship curious about the Black/white puzzle in America. M. Gimet also wanted to know about mixed marriages. "Can Negroes marry whites in your country?" was, significantly, the way he put it. I told him that interracial marriages were legal in most states and they were not so uncommon, particularly in the North. When I asked why he had inquired, he replied: "Because the Americans are racists, and we are not in France. We don't care about such things."

I thought then, as I have many times on hearing Europeans assert their claim to moral superiority in the matter of race relations, of the white man's tragic predicament in the modern world. For centuries he ruled much of the non-white world, seldom wisely or well, for he ruled solely for the benefit of his own kind, and thereby sowed a legacy of bitterness. The white men in the United States are merely Europeans removed across the Atlantic. The racism the

Europeans condemn in their American cousins is no weird fruit indigenous of American soil. It lies instead deep in the roots of Europe. Of course, it is true that America, a new world, to her own credit might have rejected racism as she rejected—in principle, at least—other institutions from the old world. But that is another matter. She did not reject it. And now those who dwell in the lands where the idea became an instrument of international policy delight in pointing an accusing finger at the land where they imported it. The suspicion that this name-calling is a way of detracting from the character of Europe's successor in world power and prestige is not mitigating. Neither taunts nor holier-than-thou poses will regain for Europe the position that her own racism helped to rob her of. And, regrettably, Europeans don't yet know that it no longer matters so terribly much who is the greater racist. They all wear the same face. And the damage was long since done.

Days later, in Guinea, another Frenchman found it necessary to parade the fiction of Frenchmen's indifference to race. This one was chief of the Conakry base of FRIA, an aluminum mining firm and the General Motors of Guinea. Lionel Debaste was a gracious and personable man whose clothes and manner seemed more suited for Paris than steamy, sticky West Africa. He made a point of being helpful. I had encountered difficulty in getting into the interior and M. Debaste took the matter in his own hands. He telephoned the Minister of Economics and Plan, Fofana Karim, and arranged an immediate appointment for me. Then he got out his car and drove me to the minister's office.

After my talk with M. Karim I found M. Debaste in Place Ballay, the little square in front of the presidential palace. Something was on his mind, and it turned out to be what he considered the difference between the French and the American attitude towards Blacks. "You see, M. Karin and I are very good friends," he said. "There is no strain in our relationship. There is no tension or fear. Tell me, can you have such friendships between whites and Negroes in America?"

It was, in a way, not so simple a question. If he was asking if there exist genuine friendships between whites and Blacks in America, the answer was yes. I have white friends. But if, on the other hand, he was asking if genuine friendships exists between corporation executives and Blacks, then my answer could only be: I don't know.

But I did not believe in M. Debaste's friendship with the African anymore than I believed M. Gimet's claim that Frenchmen are not racists. Their attitudes were too self-conscious to be genuine. And, worse, they reeked of condescension.

That morning in the park M. Debaste discussed the colonial situation and the nationalist movement in Africa which is so particularily significant for France. He said he did not oppose independence for African nations. He could understand their longings. "But all these people should realize that Europeans have done much more for them than they would've been able to do themselves." And then he took a wide swipe at an array of former subject nations—Egypt, India, Ghana, Indo-China. "Before the Europeans Came they were forever divided in tribes and religious groups, fighting and killing each other."

It was incredible hearing this urbane and experienced man dismissing the cultures of, specifically, Egypt and India, lands where great civilizations thrived when his own ancestors were primitives. But, if he could casually omit history, there seemed little profit in reminding him of it. Instead, I asked M. Debaste if putting an end to internecine warfare among Africans and Asians had been the real motive of European conquests. He considered a moment and smilingly admitted there had been less altruistic incentives. I asked him if the two great world wars of his own lifetime had been started by Asians or Africans and if—in keeping with his logic—the Indo-Chinese or Ghanaians would have been morally justified in conquering Europe to put an end to the "tribal" carnage. He laughed. He had, of course, never thought of it in that way.

M. Gimet shared M. Debaste's hypocritical view on racism and, like the elegant executive, he was also helpful. His business trips took him to all the French territories along the Atlantic, and he knew the port cities well, Conakry included. He recommended a reasonable hotel, the Niger, and a restaurant, the Paradis, where the food was both good and moderately priced. None of the Guinean soldiers I met aboard ship were able to provide any such useful information. They seemed to know as little of the physical facilities of Conakry as they did of the political organization of the country, about which they were astonishingly ignorant. No doubt out of pride and patriotism, since they had seen other cities, the Guineans did think that Conakry was a great city, an opinion not shared in the least by M. Gimet. "It's laid out like a box," he said accusingly, as if the French government-originated city plan was further proof of the inability of the Africans. "No imagination at all. Grass huts are all mixed up with the new buildings. The Africans have no standards. It's a mess."

Conakry, I discovered in time, was certainly no smaller version of Paris. It is a rather tiny land mass jutting out into the Atlantic and, with the exception of the 15-story Paternelle building, the eight-story FRIA headquarters, and the racy, Miami-style Hotel de France, is not very impressive.

The low, rectilinear presidential palace is the most attractive government building, the others of a generally flat and uninspired architecture, much like that in the so-called "banana republics." Gravel covers the rambling grounds of the palace and the walks to Place Ballay, being more practical than grass for the seven months of coastal rain. The seaside avenues and some of those in the government center are appealing, principally because of the lush palm and mango trees thoughtfully left standing when the city was carved out of the tropical jungle.

The commercial life of Guinea remains substantially in the hands of Europeans, who are so much in evidence in Conakry that they give the impression of constituting far more than a twentieth of the city's 80,000 inhabitants. There are only a few African-owned businesses of any type, the existing ones mostly small stores and shops, and their appearance tends to support M. Gimet's charge that their standards are low. Perhaps the only African-owned enterprise that would meet with M. Gimet's approval is Diop's Restaurant, a popular eating and meeting place for African intellectuals and European *afficionados* of Diop's cuisine. The rather haughty Senegalese specializes in traditional African dishes transformed to savory elegance through the adaptation of French cookery. My own experience at Diop's was, however, unhappy. Unlike the French-owned restaurants, Diop's keeps no menu and therefore provides no automatic listing of prices. I understood his reasons when he presented me with a luncheon bill exactly double what I later paid for the same meal at the French restaurant recommended by M. Gimet.

5

On the sixth day of the voyage, the sky was serene and clear all day and passengers clogged the decks. Non-commissioned officers among the African soldiers were now evident in large numbers on the deck and in the lounge. I noticed that the French soldiers chatted and jostled with the Africans on deck and drank with them at the bar. But, throughout the voyage, I never once saw the three Antillians speak to an African. They also did not seem curious about my visit to Guinea and asked no questions, although they were otherwise friendly enough. The trio remained nearly always together except when they joined the French soldiers for games or bull sessions or made a foursome at cards with a buxom, pony-tailed blonde who was especially intimate with one of them.

The following day was perfect. Cool, corrugated water and white-screened sky. Warm, calm, as clear as distilled blue water. The ship sailed through a school of porpoises cavorting like playful puppies, doing fantastic ballet leaps and turns in the air. Now and then, on either side, a lonely ship against the horizon. But no land, no land since Casablanca.

I finally had the chance to talk to Luc, the African pygmy. He was never seen on deck or in the second-class lounge, and he always vanished before I had finished eating since he was served first at a little table for two just inside the doorway. Luc was the approximate size of a 10-year-old, intelligent and friendly. He said he was the "boy" for a French family traveling first class and was enroute to Brazzaville from Marseille. He was from a Congo village where his mother still lived, and while he was not certain of his age he thought it was "around 30."

While sitting with the Whitakers in the lounge prior to going to see a Fernandel movie in the second-class dining room, Daniel arrived in his red turtle-neck sweater. He talked for awhile of his gay playboy life in Algiers, apparently forgetting he was supposed to be married. From recounting tales of lavish champagne parties in his apartment and intimate friendships with international cabaret stars, he shifted to the more serious subject of the future of Africa. "In twenty years all the whites will be driven out," he said. "Their days are numbered." And then, flashing his ever-ready grin, he regarded Syl and me with unabashed admiration. "You two are handsome like Belafonte, only Belafonte looks more like a woman," he said. "Africans are not big and broadshouldered like you. When the white men came to Africa they took all the big strong men to America as slaves and left the puny ones behind."

For a long while after the movie I stood on the moonlit deck and talked with Yao Kouame. Yao though small like Daniel, was the Senegalese's opposite in every other way. He spoke softly, carefully, and one could almost imagine his alert mind guiding his thought to the proper frame of reference and his tongue to the precise word or phrase. He spoke of politicians, of poets, of tyrants and zealots, European and African, always quietly, using his tiny, almost feminine hand to punctuate his logic as the French do. With uncommon knowledge and proficiency he discussed the American system of government, contrasting it with the French. He talked of the works of Dreiser and Faulkner and Wright and confided that he did a little writing himself, poetry and essays, and some of his work had been published. Before going below deck, he gave me pamphlets to read on French West Africa and the names of books which would illuminate the history of the political and economic development of the French-speaking territories.

Yao felt no enmity toward the French. They had done much that was evil and they had done much that was good, and it did not really matter now, at this stage, whether one outweighed the other. Africa would be ruled by Africans. Perhaps not tomorrow. But they would rule. "There is much to be done yet," he said ambiguously, and I felt I understood. I also felt that Black Africa, if she could find enough young men like Yao, was inevitably destined to add anew to the wisdom and richness of human history.

6

The Foch was docked at the huge, busy Dakar harbor when I awoke the next morning. I looked out of the porthole and saw what, at first, was a startling sight. African men in white and blue robes or in shorts scurried about the dock or stood in the shade of the giant warehouses and placidly watched. Women, wearing colors that might have been borrowed from a jazzed-up rainbow, sauntered like tranquilized panthers in the blazing sun, their heads protected by swirling swathes that matched their frocks. But it was the color of their skin that was most astounding. They looked blue-black, like glistening new steel. It was fascinating and exhilarating. I hurriedly dressed and went up on deck for a better view.

Going below again, I found Mr. Abraham filling out his police card for debarkation. He had spoiled the original card and had obtained a new one. He sat cross-legged on his bunk in deepest concentration. He had reached the question inquiring into his marital status, and he was stumped. "What should I put down?" he asked. I suggested that he simply write "not married," but that seemed to strike him as inadequate. "How do you say *celibate* in French?" he asked, and he didn't smile at all.

A small, graying African who had just come aboard heard me speaking with Mr. Abraham and came toward me, extending his hand. "Hallo," he said. "You from Ghana, sir?" I shook hands and told him I was an American. He was delighted. "An American! Ah, that's good!" He regarded me fondly, smiling. "You American, eh?" I assured him I was indeed American and asked where he was from. Gambia, he said, that little piece of imperial Britain slicing into the center of Senegal from the sea. He said he worked on the docks but that he did not earn enough money to make it worthwhile. When I told him I was going to Guinea, he said: "France is going to lose all of Africa, just like Guinea. The whites have all the good jobs and all the money. The black man has only hard work."

At Algiers, when I stepped off the gangblank onto the ground, I had paused, marking with a secret moment of solemnity the touch of my feet upon the soil of Africa. There was not, as I would have liked, some significant emotion to be afterwards associated with the occasion. And, indeed, except for the brief excursion into the Casbah, Algiers might have been a city in France or some other country along the north shore of the Mediterranean. Casablanca was more African, but only because the Moroccans were more in evidence in the streets and shops and ordinary service jobs. The bazaars and markets and medinahs, like tourist traps, did not appreciably alter the French—and therefore European—character of the city.

But Dakar, for me, was Africa. Perhaps not the Africa of Solomon and Abyssinia and Egypt, of Hannibal and the old Roman Empire, but the Africa evoked by the word as it is popularly used in America. The "dark" continent, the source of slaves and tribes and beasts and jungles and fever. A word rife with negative connotations. At first I could see only the people. There was about them a surpassing serenity. A serenity and a sureness. It began to be clear to me that an element of their visual mysteriousness was the absence in their faces of the indelible imprint of harassment and fear and of their counter reactions, sullenness and combativeness, emotions that haunt the Black American. It was with joy that I watched the women on the streets, moving like so many ebony monarchs, their heads high, their shoulders straight, their backs slightly swayed, their hips swinging free and sinuously as if to some voluptuous inner music. Of course, I knew the origin of their grace. There they were on the streets and in the markets, balancing burdens effortlessly on their heads. And the vivid, almost screeching colors that they bustled and skirted and draped like saris about their bodies were right for them, perfect. Dark-skinned Black American women are intimidated by brilliant colors. They turn their backs on them. For the aquamarines and tangerines and fuschias would call attention to their skin, and that would never do! In America, one does not accentuate one's blackness; one tries to hide it beneath creams and paints and powders. And failing that, one plays it down with quiet, dark and neutral colors, appropriately matched with a bland, apologetic manner.

But one understands their shyness. For the Black American, all his years on the American continent, has been fleeing the color he associates with his shame. He has been running from the color which forever marks him, in his imposed language and religion, as not quite a man. One understands this. One understands when a friend's mother, learning her son wants to marry a dark-skinned girl, threatens to take poison if he does. "Think of the children," she moaned. "They will be black." And one understands when a co-worker, regarding a fair-skinned, straight-haired little girl, says, "Now that's a fine example of selective breeding." And what he meant, what Blacks in America go on proving, is that the fairer the skin and the straighter the hair the closer they come to feeling whole.

When I worked as a newspaper reporter in Detroit, the white director of an adoption agency, speaking in innocence of a near-white baby among a group of dark-skinned ones, said, "That baby is the most popular. Six or seven couples want to adopt her. It's so strange. I think several of the others are so much sweeter, but no one seems to want them." One understands this self-hatred without giving it any sympathy.

The Africans of Dakar were a revelation. But there was also this unexpected new city. Dakar is large and rambling, much of it built since the end of World War II. The territorial assembly and some of the government buildings are among the most modern and attractive I have seen anywhere; the commercial center of tall banks and offices is constructed around a sunny plaza; the international airport is an important link in the ever-expanding air traffic between Europe and South America; and the new University of Dakar, the only institution of higher learning in the vast French West Africa area, aspires to replace the world-renowned Sorbonne as the educational and cultural mecca of French-speaking Africa.

But Dakar also has some of the world's worst slums. Later, in Conakry, during one of my several talks with Sékou Touré, he spoke of the Dakar slums, opening another window on French accomplishments in the city in the past 15 years. "Yes, the French have built a magnificent harbor, a great airdrome, skyscrapers and boulevards," he said. "But this serves and enriches the Europeans and has brought virtually no benefits to 90 percent of the people. In terms of progress for Senegal, the modern look of Dakar is an illusion. You have only to look at the terrible poverty in the suburbs and in the heart of the city to see what I mean."

On my return to Europe I spent two days in Dakar and

had a fresh look at the city. There was much to what Touré had said. There are fewer than a handful of Senegalese in the blocks of handsome new apartment buildings with balconies overlooking the sea. And it is rare to see an African sitting at the tables of the downtown sidewalk cafes. Not because they would be refused, for that would be unthinkable. Rather because the African middle class is so small and the African leisure class as yet nonexistent.

One of the pleasanter surprises of Dakar was the U.S. Information Service office there. It is located a few blocks from the center of town in a bright new building. Its director, a Mr. Jacoby, is an eloquent man with great enthusiasm for his work. His chief assistant at the time was Bill Dixon, a young man from Montclair, New Jersey, who had recently left a similar post in Athens. Several weeks earlier the U.S.I.S. had sponsored a lecture on "Negro" literature in the U.S. by Miss Naomi Garrett, a Black professor of romance languages at West Virginia State College. Both Mr. Jacoby and Mr. Dixon lavished praise on Miss Garrett's handling of what must have been a difficult situation during the question and answer session following the lecture. " The African students can be very rambunctious," Mr. Jacoby said. "They came prepared to tear her limb from limb if she tried to smooth over the racial situation at home. They asked rather pointed questions about racial discrimination, but Miss Garret never lost her poise. She also didn't pull any punches. She related all the bitterness and protest that go into Negro literature."

I could imagine some of the students' attitudes. Weeks later, in Conakry, I found myself similarly cornered. While dining with a party of Guineans I was introduced to a rather majestic postal worker in Moslem robes. The man regarded me with elaborate disdain and immediately said: "Tell us about racial segregation in America." Unprepared for this attack, I hesitated a moment, deciding how and in what mood to meet it. Equanimity seemed the best approach, so I proceeded with the conventional background information. "Well, in America, the states of the South have traditionally . . ." But that was as far as I got. "What difference does it make where the states are?" he snapped. "It is still America, isn't it?"

Many African intellectuals, possibly through envy, the same motive prompting much European criticism of American whites, delight in twisting the blade of racial ostracism protruding from the heart of Black Americans' citizenship. It can be painful. These Africans assume a superior pose because they now know, even when they are colonials, that their ascendancy to power is only a matter of time. And also, they are in their own lands, on their own continent, and they can never be made to feel as aliens.

I asked Mr. Jacoby of Leopold Senghor, Senegal's brilliant poet-statesman and the territory's deputy in the Parliament at Paris. Mr. Jacoby said that Senghor was indeed in town, representing Senegal at the Constituent Assembly currently drawing up a constitution joining Senegal, Dahomey, Sudan and Haute Volta in a federated state. With the Whitakers, I went searching for Senghor at the impressive new territorial assembly hall but had no luck tracking him down. The assembly adopted a constitution creating Mali, after an ancient West African empire, I learned after arriving at Conakry. However, Dahomey and Haute Volta later withdrew from the federation, and all four territories became autonomous republics within the French "community."

That evening, as the boat pulled out of the harbor and I began the final lap of my journey, I noted a marked change in the demeanor of the African soldiers. Until Dakar, they had seemed shy and withdrawn, though decreasingly so, seldom noisy or obtrusive. But now they swarmed all over the ship, even below deck to use the electric iron reserved for second and third class passengers and the rest rooms of the two classes. Also, in a reversal of behavior, the white passengers moved about with apparent trepidation, almost furtively, peering into lounges or loitering uncomfortably on the decks. Long before midnight, when the soldiers' laughter and singing was loudest, the whites had all but vanished from the decks and salons.

7

The next day I saw young Keita Faraban for the first time since Algiers. When he approached, I was standing alone on deck trying to sight land through the curious haze between the ship and the shore. "I've been looking everywhere for you," he said. I had, from time to time, sought him out in the hope that he might be able to give me an idea of what to expect in Conakry. It was a surprise to have him look for me. "Come, I want to show you something," he said, rather mysteriously. I followed him along the deck to the marker of the first-class promenade where he stopped. He seemed afraid of passing beyond, although there were no physical barriers. He pointed toward the prow. "Go and look," he said. "You will see how the African soldiers live."

I had not been to that end of the ship since the evening of Algiers, just after the soldiers came aboard, and I remembered thinking there were a great many of them and wondering casually where they would sleep. I understood there was a steerage section on the ship but I had not been curious enough to seek it out. I walked to the head of the deck, leaned over the railing, and looked down upon the most dismaying sight of the voyage.

Below, and on the raised section beyond, hundreds of soldiers milled about in all stages and varieties of dress and undress. Among them, sitting on their haunches, lying across freight, soiled mattresses and household furnishings, or snaking through the maggoty mob, were dozens of civilians—men, women and children. It was lunch time and a line was discernible outside a hutlike structure on the deck below. Soldiers and women held assorted containers which someone in the hut filled with great gobs of rice dotted with hunks of meat. Groups squatted around pots and buckets filled with food, eating with their fingers. Discarded beer cans and soda water bottles served as community drinking vessels. The floors were wet and slippery with garbage, orange and banana peels.

I climbed down the steps and crept close enough to look inside the hut that was apparently the kitchen. It was dark and junky, crowded with great smoky vats. I saw a cook, stripped to the waist, pour the drippings of cooked fish over a bucket of rice which he passed to a soldier. Opposite the kitchen, a door led to the toilets, and a terrible odor floated out from it.

When I mounted to the first-class deck again, a Frenchman was bending over the railing, looking down on the scene. He glanced at me and shook his head *"C'est formidable!"* he said. I said I thought it appalling. He laughed at that. "It is what they are accustomed to," he said.

Later I asked Yao Kouame if he had seen the spectacle on the prow and, smiling in his half-embarrassed way, he said he had. *"Ça, c'est colonialisme!"*

It was my last night aboard ship and I went below early to get everything packed and in order. The cabin attendant had left two towels exactly twice as many as he had dispensed from Palma to Dakar. He had not once changed the beds.

Nor had he ever done more in the room than make the beds. Mr. Abraham and I had, between us, kept the sink and floor clean. But we had not been inclined to clean the shower room across the passage, and it had therefore not been touched. Soap wrappers that were on the floor when I boarded the ship were still there the morning I debarked.

It had been oppressively warm, even at night, since Dakar, and the air seemed to become furnace-hot as the ship neared Conakry. I had moved my bedding to the bunk under the porthole, Mr. Abraham's former station, to benefit from any wanton breeze. Toward morning, sticky with sweat, finally fell asleep.

8

I was awakened by inept-sounding martial music and looked out the porthole to see that the ship had docked. The cabin was a hothouse. After braving the shower room I dressed and went above to discover the reason for the music. A small, winter-uniformed band was standing in formation in the sun, playing a welcome serenade to the homecoming troops. The French, I had read, had taken everything but a brass band when they quit the country in a huff. Perhaps this was the band they had left behind. A ramp had been lowered from the bow and soldiers, carrying suitcases, loose clothing, boxes and musical instruments, marched to the dock and fell into formation. They looked miserable and disreputable in the heavy uniforms and with their untidy burdens. They had been mustered out of the colonial army and would not be absorbed in their country's tiny garrison of 2,000 men. None of those I had talked to had any idea of what they would do.

When the Guinean custom officers came aboard I took my police card and passport into the salon. Only a handful of Europeans were debarking, although many later went ashore to see the city. Two Frenchmen were reluctant to get in the line behind the Africans and did so only after the customs officers refused to consider them ahead of the others. It was necessary to leave my passport, and I was told I could collect it at the *prefecture* the following morning. It was Sunday, and there was a stillness, a deadness about the day. Number-bearing porters came aboard and I selected the tallest, strongest-looking one I saw. He was a big, handsome fellow, with great muscular arms and legs. Apparently, I mused, recalling Daniel's explanation of his own smallness of stature, this porter's ancestors had escaped the slave traders. I had two large suitcases, a smaller one filled with books, a typewriter, an attache case, a toilet kit and an overcoat. With a kindly assist from Yao, we got all the luggage down the gangplank and into the customs shed in one trip.

Then my troubles began. I asked the porter how much I owed him and he said 600 francs. It was incredible. I told him I wouldn't pay it. He fumed and pawed the ground like an angry bull. I regretted having chosen such a strapping fellow. I took out 600 francs and offered them to him, but he wouldn't touch the money. "French francs are worth only half African francs," he informed me. I knew this already, but I hadn't supposed he meant African francs. That made his demands doubly incredible. I protested, turning to the onlookers in mute appeal for support or sympathy, but none was forthcoming. The Africans watched the little scene with elaborate neutrality. "Pay me!" the porter demanded. "Or I'll have to take your bags back to the boat."

I offered the 600 francs again. This time he slobbered and stamped and shouted what must have been epithets in a language I'd never heard, trembling with rage. I decided to compromise. I offered another 400 French francs and told him emphatically he wouldn't get more. He snatched the money and trotted off through the huge empty building back to the ship. At black market exchange rates, I had paid him $2 to bring two suitcases down the gangplank. I had been taken.

Customs formalities took only a minute. The agent asked if I had anything to declare, and I said no. He seemed relieved. I looked about for a taxi and, seeing none on the grounds, asked the customs agent how I could get one. Taxis, he informed me, were not allowed through the port gates unless they had passengers. There possibly were taxis outside the gates and the gates were—he stepped to the door to show me—around the bend and about 800 meters further on.

One of the Africans near the doorway cozied up and offered to get a taxi. He was young and strong but not so big and capable looking as the porter. "How long will it take?" I asked him. He said he didn't know. If there wasn't one, then he would have to go and find one. "I can carry your luggage to the gates," he said. "Only 250 francs." African, of course. There didn't seem to be another way, so I agreed. With the aid of a bystander, the African balanced the two large suitcases on his head and took the smaller one in his right hand. Sweat rolled like rain from his face. He reached for the typewriter, but I kept it. I couldn't believe he could walk all that distance with that great weight on his head.

But he did. The guards at the gates noted the customs marks on the luggage and permitted him to pass without lowering it. An old, shabby-looking Buick sedan with "taxi" crudely painted on the side was parked beside a taxi marker across the street. When we reached it, the driver said he was waiting for a passenger. She soon appeared, a great black Senegalese, waddling imperiously across the plaza, her orchid sari flowing, her head erect, an orange stick between her teeth. Behind her loped several men bearing her belongings —one of the mattresses I had seen on the bow, assorted pieces of furniture and a battered pasteboard suitcase. The men somehow attached this property to the taxi, they all climbed inside, and the muddy machine rattled off toward the city.

There are taxis in Conakry, a fleet owned by a Frenchwoman. The vehicles are clean and new, the drivers careful and courteous. However, the taxis are either hired at the headquarters or dispatched by phone, and do not cruise the streets. All this I learned later. Being ignorant of this at the time, I waited with the porter for nearly half an hour before another free-lance "taxi" appeared. In the meantime, the porter tried to persuade me to let him carry the luggage on his head to the Hotel du Niger. "For the same 250 francs?" I asked. "For the same price," he said. But I refused. I did not relish the idea of trudging through the streets in that enervating heat with a typewriter, attache case, toilet kit and overcoat, with no prior knowledge of how far I had to carry them.

When the other "taxi" arrived, it was promptly claimed by an African who was at the taxi stand when we got there. He argued and bargained with the driver and, apparently unable to arrive at suitable terms, passed the taxi on to me.

How much to the Hotel du Niger?" I asked the driver. He answered 400 francs. Then I discovered that I had only French francs left and the porter would not accept them. "They'll exchange them at the hotel," he said, climbing uninvited into the taxi. The outbidded Senegalese stuck his head in the window and asked if I would allow him to ride into town. I told him he could ride as far as I went. He climbed in too.

The Hotel du Niger was, in fact, only a few blocks

away, and the porter might easily have negotiated the distance with the luggage on his head. We drove through a small, deserted square dominated by a lonely statue on a pedestal in the shadow of a giant fromager tree that looked as ancient as the California sequoias. I never saw the statue again. A few days later, a team of husky laborers ripped down the monuments to Guinea's colonial past. It was not a troublesome task. The only two such memorials in the city stood in the center of Place Ballay in front of the presidential palace. Both men had been colonial governors of the territory.

There was no movement along the taxi route, except for an occasional dog or chicken darting across the street from one of the sleeping, dust-covered, low-roofed houses. The taxi turned and suddenly activity exploded in the street. Hordes of people, mostly women, sashayed along the unpaved sidewalk, stopping to gossip or to haggle with the vendors behind portable stalls. The women of coastal Guinea are a rich cocoa color, tall and stately, gayer and less imperious than the Senegalese. They carry great white basins on their heads and, often, babies bandaged on their hips. I found it amazing that the babies, borne piggy-back in that fashion until they can walk, never seem to cry. They look out on the world with solemn faces, content and undemanding.

Behind the sidewalk vendors, a block deep, sprawled a labyrinthine system of stalls and stands where everything from herbs to clothing was on sale. In the middle of all this, rising like some free-form concrete modern monster above the straw roofs of the stalls, was the concrete central city market, replete with ramps, featuring such innovations as snack bars with kitchens and dining areas where short orders and delicacies were concocted and eaten. An exotic, piercingly pungent smell, redolent of dried fish and garlic, wafted from the market. It was strong and sour and the air of the city was never entirely free of it.

The taxi turned another corner and abruptly stopped in front of a long, drab three-story building fronted by a restaurant. I looked questioningly at the porter and he said, "This is the Hotel du Niger." Already harassed and weary and limp, I tasted despair. The restaurant was large, clean, attractively paneled and cool-looking, but it had nothing in common with the building above and around it. The hotel looked like a flea-den along Chicago's South State Street. I wondered if M. Gimet had played a malicious joke on me.

Regarding my fallen face, the driver suggested that we go on to the Hotel de France. I was tempted, but I remembered the low level of my funds. According to M. Gimet, rooms at the Hotel de France began at 1800 francs a day, nearly $8. I asked the driver to wait and went in the restaurant to find the hotel clerk. There was one customer at the bar, drinking beer, and a short, Italianate man behind the counter. I asked the bartender if there were rooms in the hotel. He said no. There was a big conference of some kind ("Something to do with the labor movement," he said, shrugging) in town. It ended today. Perhaps at noon. . . . How much? Fifteen hundred francs a day. When I looked surprised, he said: "Nice rooms, with showers. Very nice." M. Gimet's information was that Hotel du Niger rooms were 800 francs a day. Half that. Well, even at 1500 francs I would be saving more than a dollar a day, and if the hotel was unbearable, I would simply have to go on to the Hotel de France. The bartender gave me African francs for French ones, I paid the porter and the driver and stacked my luggage in a corner of the restaurant.

Noon was almost two hours away. I went for a walk, taking the opposite direction from the hectic market. All the dust-sprayed commercial buildings were closed and barred. Only a few people were on the streets. Toward the pier, beyond the tops of spreading mango trees, loomed the city's skyscraper, the 15-story Paternelle building. Like most new structures, it served as both office and living quarters for European firms and personnel. The character of the city was much as M. Gimet had described it. Modern apartment buildings overlooked African-style compounds, including occasionlly bee-hive shaped huts. And, unlike Yao's Abidjan, there was no residential segregation, racial nor economic.

I decided to go to the Hotel de France and check on its prices. I asked the first person I saw—a young man in white shirt and dark slacks—how to get there. "I'm sorry, but I don't speak French," he answered in English. He was Sierra-Leonan, from Freetown. He had a few minutes free and would walk me to the hotel. Arthur was a postal worker using up some of his accumulated leave. "There's no place to go, and furthermore I don't have any money," he said dourly. He was soft-spoken but voluble and talked in a charming accent reminiscent of the British West Indies. He thought Sierra Leone was backward and blamed the leadership of the British colony, old men with little imagination or industry. "Now they're spending a lot of money to receive the Queen when she visits Africa this fall," he said. "It's a lot of nonsense. What do we need the Queen for?"

While Arthur was critical of his own country and its leaders, he was glad Sierra Leone was not as "foolish" as Liberia. "I don't like Monrovia at all," he declared. "They are lunatics. They all behave as if they just discovered Europe." Arthur had accompanied an aunt to Conakry to consult a French physician. Why, I asked, did she come so far to see the doctor? "The Sierra Leonans prefer French doctors," he shrugged. "They are fools."

The Hotel de France, perhaps the most attractive building in Guinea, nestles on a small rise at the point of two converging avenues and overlooks the sea. It is framed by gigantic mango and palm trees and has a dining room that projects over a garden gay with tropical flowers and favored by wild white birds that look like miniature storks. An assortment of adventurers, journalists, entrepreneurs, businessmen and envoys, primarily Eastern European, loitered about the lounge and the dining room, for the sun outdoors was fierce and there was little diversion elsewhere. The clerk affirmed M. Gimet's quotation of prices and, anyway, none of the cheaper rooms were available.

I crossed the hotel garden and seaside drive and stood a moment on the seawall. The misty Isles of Loos lay offshore, and a large barge rested in a distant cove. The isles, like vast areas on the mainland, are rich in minerals, principally bauxite, which, washed into shore, have colored the huge craggy boulders in the surf a rusty, funeral brown. Great shaggy vultures and birds the size of chicken hawks but with the heads of doves hover over the coast and perch mournfully on the rocks, adding to the coastal air of doom and decay.

I walked along the shore, past a casino with fenced-in grounds and a beach where European families lay sunning. Further on, bordering a fishing pier, stood another, a smaller, market, under an open concrete pavilion. Across the street rose a pair of seven-story apartment buildings. The balconies were cluttered and hung with dingy and faded clothing.

Someone called out, "Hallo," and I turned to see two Africans in shorts coming toward me from the market. I stopped and waited. One was small, like Yao and Daniel, the other taller, broader, husky. The little one did all the talking, smiling, always smiling, as if his face automatically

A Journey to Africa

snapped into that unoffending mask. "Are you English?" he asked. It was the first time I had ever been asked that or, for that matter, the first time I knew there were people who thought of Black people as being English. But many Guineans later asked the same question, and I even met Nigerians in Conarky who said they were English.

The little man had the same calypso-flavored accent as Arthur and was, in fact, from Sierra-Leone. He and his companion had been left behind by a Dutch ship on which they had signed up at Monrovia. They had come ashore while the ship was in port, had drunk too much beer, and had arrived back at the pier too late. They had no money and no place to stay and had been sleeping on the beach. Could I help them? I couldn't. I actually had only a few hundred francs left, and they had to keep me until I could cash a traveler's check.

The stranded sailors had met the day before another "American black man," they said, a magazine photographer, and he had given them money. "A nice gentleman." I was extremely curious about the Black American photographer and, despite my having no money to give them, they took me to where they thought he was stopping. It was a minor government official's house on a low cliff above the sea, but the photographer did not live there. No one knew where he was. The next day I met the "American black man" at the telegraph office. He was a Ghanaian working with Curt Prendergast, *Time* magazine's African correspondent who was gathering material for the February 16 cover story on Sékou Touré and Guinea.

Hot, sweaty and a little sick, I found my way back to the hotel. There was a room. The *patron* led me out of the restaurant, to the end of the corner, and down the street beside the hotel building. "But we're passing the hotel," I said, somewhat alarmed, for the buildings on the side street were even shabbier than the hotel. "No, the rooms there are all filled," he assured me. "We're going to the annex."

It was not until days later that I discovered that the hotel to which the bartender-patron led me was not at all an "annex" to the Hotel du Niger but a new hotel which he owned. Unknown to the management of the Hotel du Niger, this man was receiving people who wandered, as I did, into his restaurant thinking it was the main floor of the hotel. It was easy to make this assumption. The restaurant was large and extended out over the sidewalk while the entrance to the hotel was an unmarked doorway a hundred feet away that was easy to overlook. The Hotel du Niger, deceptively, was clean, orderly and well-run, and its prices were as M. Gimet had quoted them. The new hotel was later baptised the Savoie.

Even had I known this at the time I doubt it would have mattered. I was too weak and weary to protest. Whatever the place was like, I thought, I could always change the next day. I needed to get somewhere and lie down. Anywhere. At the end of the block, the *patron* opened a makeshift gate and ushered me into a small, mosaic-paved courtyard and up a flight of outside steps. It was a new building, an unfinished building in fact, for only the floor to which he took me was completed. It had eight large rooms, all with new furnishings, and with showers and all the cold running water one could use. I slumped gratefully across the bed and slept.

9

I was awakened by an American voice outside my door wrestling bravely but not very successfully with the French language. I dashed to the door and swung it open. In the hallway with the attendant stood a tall, middle-aged Black

American. He was, for some reason, a comforting sight. He came in and sat down and we discovered we were both from Detroit. Vernon Yarbrough, owner of a small restaurant-hotel business, was a former follower of the late Marcus Garvey, the West Indian-born Harlemite who wanted to lead Black Americans back to Africa. Mr. Yarbrough had been in Africa since December, had attended the historically important African Peoples' conference in Accra and had come to Conakry from Monrovia.

He liked Ghana and found it inspiring, a belated realization of Garvey's dreams, I surmised. On the other hand, he thought Liberia a joke that, like the nigger stories of the Old South, was not only passé but mocking to those involved with it. "Why, they'll dress up in soup-and-fish at the drop of a hat!" he said. "And after 100 years of freedom, the bigshots haven't done a thing to develop and improve the country. It's just a big Firestone plantation."

And what did he think of Conakry? "It's too expensive!" was the quick reply. He liked the mood and pace of the city and the quality of mind of the Africans he had talked with, but Mr. Yarbrough was not even going to stay to investigate business possibilities in Guinea. He had arrived on Friday, had been stood up on an appointment with a minister, and was taking the evening plane to Dakar and on the Paris. He expected to be home in Detroit on Wednesday. He promised to telephone my family.

Though I felt better after a nap and the chat with Mr. Yarbrough, I still felt out of sorts. I decided that a shower and shave and another walk might help. This time I took a different route, past the market and down the broad, divided Boulevard Charles de Gaulle. There were more people about in the afternoon, women in their gorgeous headdress and bouffant tunics over long, flowered sarongs, men in starched robes or white shirt and carefully pressed trousers. The Europeans were abroad too, driving small, jeep-like autos or gossiping under the terraces of the sidewalk cafes.

Conakry is bordered on three sides by the sea, and I soon reached the coast again. A moment later a car stopped beside me and an African with a kindly schoolteacher's face pushed his head out of the window and offered me a lift. The driver was Bengaly Camara, Guinea's Minister of Labor. When I introduced myself, he apparently assumed I had come as a journalist to cover the conference that had filled the hotels. "The meetings are all over now," he told me. "Everyone is at the stadium."

I had no idea what he was talking about, but I thought it advisable to discover what was going on in an indirect manner. I explained that I had only just arrived that morning and had found it necessary to rest. "Well, it's too bad you're so late, but I'll get you the literature and someone will drive you to the field."

M. Camara drove to the Bousre de Travail, a handsome seaside building originally designed as an outdoor theater. A worker was mimeographing pamphlets and bulletins, and I was given a handful. Glancing through them, I learned that the General Congress of the General Union of Black African Workers (U.G.T.A.N.) had just concluded its sessions. The union, claiming 700,000 members in the French African territories, had elected as president its ablest helmsman, Sékou Touré. This must surely have marked the first time in history that the head of an independent nation had accepted the chieftainship of an international labor union.

M. Camara delivered me into the custody of a thin, strained-looking young man name Khole and instructed him to drive me to the outdoor stadium where a huge public celebration in honor of the congress was in progress. I followed Khole outside to a new maroon Aronde sedan. A dainty African girl in yellow organdy was waiting in the rear seat. Khole introduced us, and she smiled prettily, shaking hands. Her name was Assi. She and Khole asked a few polite questions and then took up the trail of a discussion that my appearance had interrupted. The gist of it seemed to be that the festival had been sloppily planned, *"pas bein organisé,"* as Assi kept repeating.

Khole drove a few blocks and stopped, parking at the entrance to one of the project-style compounds characteristic of the city. A passage, as wide as a driveway, opened between two houses on the street and led into a large communal square completely bordered by other houses. It is the bush village translated into an urban pattern. Khole begged our leave and entered the compound, returning a few minutes later wearing a white robe. In Conakry, as in Dakar, simple white or blue robes are worn by men at least as regularly as Western clothing. It is estimated that 70 percent of Guineans are Moslems.

Khole drove like a jeep-jockey around the curving seaside drive and over the neck of the peninsula out of the city. The highway was in good condition, but narrow, and fortunately there was very little traffic meeting us. There were many people on foot or on bicycles traveling in our direction, however, and several were forced to flee for their lives as the red machine bore down on them. We sped past villages of thatched huts, factories, new shopping centers roughly reminiscent of those in U.S. suburbs, and long stretches of parched land. At length the traffic and crowds along the highway grew denser, finally all but impassable. Khole cleared a passage by leaning on his horn and refusing at any time to bring the car to a full halt. Knee-trousered policemen tried desperately to keep the street clear but had much less success than Khole.

Arriving at last at the gate, Khole yelled to the guards that his passenger was an American whom he had orders to take directly to Sékou Touré. The ruse worked admirably. Miraculously, the guards forced a wedge through the solid mass of squirming, sweating people. Khole parked the Aronde beside a sleek 1959 royal blue DeSoto which I later learned was a gift to Touré from President Tubman of Liberia. We climbed out of the oven-hot car onto the ground where the heat was searing and Khole turned me over to a guard. "Escort monsieur l'Américain to President Touré."

This, I thought, was carrying the ruse a bit far and I turned to Khole to protest, but he waved me on. The guard motioned that I should follow him and we burrowed toward the sound of voices bellowing into loudspeakers. We reached a roped-off area with a natural earth mound in the center on which close to 100 important-looking people, black and white, sat on folding chairs. There was no canopy, no protection from the terrible sun. Sékou Touré, in a brown winter-weight suit and yellow-brown tie, occupied the center chair on the front row. In front of him, on a platform, a slender Guinean spieled French into a raised microphone. In front of this speaker, on another platform in the surf of the sea of people, another Guinean shouted into another microphone, translating the first speaker's words into Soussou, the language of the chief tribe of Guinea's coastal region.

The guard lifted the rope and invited me to slip under it. Then he led me directly to Sékou Touré. "M. President, an American visitor." Touré raised his eyes, stared probingly, and allowed the hint of a smile to cross his ruggedly handsome face. He shook hands firmly, nodding, murmuring something I could not understand. There were two empty chairs two seats away, probably reserved for the two men at the microphones. I sat in the nearest one.

It was dehydratingly hot. I had never been so hot in my life. My clothing was completely soaked, my throat arid, my eyes glazed and burning. An awful fear that I might be messily sick gripped me. I tried to dismiss the fear, knowing the thought is father of the deed. I concentrated on Touré. He sat motionless, erect, looking out over the crowd like some serene divinity beyond the influence of the debilitating sun.

In my four subsequent meetings with Touré, I found him equipped with a great natural talent for histrionics. His shrewd mind, honed to brilliance in the treacherous arenas of colonial politics and Marxist-dominated labor unions, forever flashes, sifts, weighs, maneuvers. He knows he must be many things to many people, and he is master of all his different roles. He is aloof or warm or simply straightforward or subtle, as he feels the occasion demands. And he can be several of these things within a matter of minutes.

On my first visit to Touré's office, he received me behind his neat, modest desk beneath a huge framed photograph of himself and Ghana's Kwame Nkrumah on the occasion of the Ghana-Guinea "union" a month after Guinea's independence. He neither rose nor smiled but shook my hand from his seat, keeping the searching, measuring eyes on my face. Throughout the interview he remained distant, cool, answering most questions with a single word or phrase.

But the next time I was granted an interview, he came

toward me from behind the desk, smiling and asked, "And how is our American friend today?" He threw a comradely arm around my shoulder and led me to the window. Standing there, looking through the branches of the great fromager tree and over the palace grounds to the sea, Touré spoke confidingly of Guinea and her many problems and of his hopes for the country and for all of Africa. He switched abruptly from this genial pose when his secretary darted into the room to announce in an excited whisper that the American consul-general from Dakar was on his way up the stairs. Touré strode to his desk and arranged himself behind it, and the American who entered a moment later was greeted by a head of state, all charm and dignity.

There on the open-air platform, when the ceremonies were finally ended and the thunderous tension of the crowd released, Touré spared a moment to act out yet another role. He paused before stepping down from the mound to greet two little boys who sneaked under the ropes and ran to him. For the first time since I had been watching him, his grave, furrowed expression relaxed, and he smiled. He shook the small hands and let his own hand rest briefly— as if in benediction—on each boy's head. Then he turned away and led the official procession to the waiting cars.

But all this occurred later. Now, as the speakers sounded off, Touré sat stolidly in the sun, facing 30,000 Guineans who had poured themselves onto the football fields, some walking the eight miles to the stadium, in order to pay him homage. He was their leader, unquestioningly, the man on whose word they rejected, by an overwhelming 95 percent vote, the status of French territory, not knowing all that their action implied and portended, but trusting in him. In their African minds—minds conditioned by centuries of tribal life in which a single man of strength, or a council of such men, ruled without challenge and, indeed, with the implicit mandate of the ruled—Touré's eminence and authority were both right and just. Sékou Touré was in his broad-shouldered, silver-tongued person the new-era embodiment of their traditional leader. If he had not been strong, if he had not contrived to eliminate or absorb all opposition, the people would not have believed in him. They would not have adored him.

All this Touré knew. It was evident that he knew it, that he could depend on his people's loyalty when, on response to the young man at the nearest microphone, he stood up. He remained quite still a moment, staring out at the sweating crowd, and only when the silence was deepest did he begin to speak. Briefly, briskly, in precisely articulated French that many of his listeners scarcely understood, he thanked the congress delegates for choosing him their leader and explained the labor union's importance for Guinea and all Africa ("There must be no exploitation of African workers!")

Then, scowling fiercely and throwing back his head, he shouted: *"Vive l'Independance!"*

The answer, amplified by 30,000 voices, rolled across the dusty, sweat-scented plain. "Vive l'Independance!"

Touré raised his head again. "Vive l'Afrique!"

And all of Africa seemed to scream back from the human sea around him. "Vive l'Afrique!"

Less than two hours later, in the gilt and chandeliered ballroom of the mansion designed for French governors, I witnessed still another Touré. Handsome in evening clothes, he stood beside his statuesque, honey-skinned wife, product of commingled strains of France and Guinea, and he was all grace. He shook hands and chatted warmly with everyone. He seemed to know all the Africans and many of the

Europeans by name. I wondered fleetingly, observing the watchful Europeans and civil servants as they moved somewhat stiffly, cautiously, among the dark-suited black men and their gayly costumed women, what thoughts lay behind their bland smiles and polite words. Were they remembering the time, not yet half a year past, when the occupants of that mansion and the host at such receptions had been of their own kind? And were they regretting?

On the way back to the hotel I thought I found perhaps the arrow of an answer. Only a pointer, for there are some 5,000 Europeans among the 80,000 people in the environs of Conakry, and their opinions and feelings about Guinea's independence must have as many variations and shadings as their number. I stopped for a drink in a small bar on the corner, a block from my hotel. The *patron* was a tall, matinee-handsome man of French-African ancestry, with intelligent gray eyes and thick, wavy black hair. He was, I learned subsequently, son of a French merchant and a Guinea beauty, and was himself married to a Frenchwoman. He sat behind the counter giving directions to his African bartender while changing the records on his pick-up. There were four customers in the bar, three Europeans standing together near the *owner* and an African alone at the far end of the counter.

When I ordered a beer the Frenchmen noticed my accent and stopped talking to observe me. One of them asked in English if I was American. Then he began to talk and to ask other questions, feeling me out. He was Jewish, he pointedly told me, intending this information as proof of his lack of prejudice. He had lived in America, in California and New York, had served in the American army during the war, he said. "What do you think of Guinea's independence?" he finally got around to asking. I told him I thought it was a good thing. "It came too soon," he said. "They don't know what they are doing. There's nothing but confusion."

Then he described how Africans who had previously lived only in wattle huts had made slums of the city's new apartment buildings. He said that where the postal service had once run engine-smooth, it was now necessary to wait in line as much as twenty minutes in order to buy stamps (it was irritatingly true). He said the Africans had no experience in running a water system, an electrical plant and planning industrial development. He turned to the caramel-colored man behind the bar and, in French, solicited his corroboration. The bar owner, speaking in clear, elegant French, agreed that the Africans had made a mistake in choosing independence so impulsively. "Guinea is my home," he said. "It has possibilities. I don't want to see it ruined." The other two Frenchmen insisted that they had nothing against Africans. They simply felt the Africans were not ready for the responsibility of government.

It all sounded so familiar. I had heard it all before so many times, too many times. In America, in Europe, in Africa. The same refrain on the lips of white men everywhere. Pathetic, violence-breeding, wishful thinking. Horace Greeley, in the *New York Tribune* of 1868, had explained it all so well. "It is difficult to argue with a blind, besotted prejudice, grounded in ignorance and fortified by self-conceit," he had wirtten of the post-Civil War racists. "Devoid of reason, is hardly amenable to reason. . . . Allow today the plea that the Blacks are ignorant and degraded, and those whom you thereby clothe with power will take good care that the plea shall be as valid and well grounded a century hence as it is now."

"Wait," they always say. "Not ready!" they cry. Why was it that, after more than half a century of French domination, there were no Africans trained to handle technical and administrative jobs? It was a reasonable question, but such opinions are "hardly amenable to reason," so I did not ask it. Instead, I said simply: "When do you think the Africans will be ready?"

There was no immediate reply. And when answers came, no definite ones. "It takes time. . . ."

But Sékou Touré had already made their reply superfluous. In assuming the role of premier he had said, in effect, that having responsibility was the best way of learning it. And the time to learn it was now.

I walked back to the hotel past dark sleeping houses from which subdued voices sounded from the open verandahs. Beneath a mango tree on the corner opposite the hotel a group of boys chanted to the music of a delicate-voiced cora, a banjo-like instrument made from a gourd. The chanting reminded me of my grandmother humming some now-forgotten song as I lay in the porch swing at twilight with my head in her lap. The rhythm had crossed the Atlantic with the slaves and, as indestructible as their genes, had refused to die.

If I had not been fully certain in the beginning, I knew then, without qualification, that my journey to Africa had only to be with my being a black man from America. It is a melancholy truth that the simple fact of that identity can inflict upon the psyche so deep a wound that a lifetime will not heal it. I had come in search of medication, and I felt I had discovered balm. My journey to Africa was merely the logical extension of my journey to Europe. I had come seeking the answer to how I could face the lacerating racial whirlwind and yet make a life in America.

The African emergence is a significant development for all the world, but it has a very special importance for those of African blood who are rooted in the American culture. For, with all respect to the moral intent of desegregation, only Africa will set the Black American free. American whites could unbind the Blacks. But they will not because, though they can soothe their consciences and gain grace by confessing their sins against us, they cannot forgive us for forcing them to live a lie.

That is, after all, the real meaning of the "Negro problem." The Negro stands in innocence at the center of white America's self-betrayal. The Black man has merely to exist, to be, to provoke a frenzy of sacrilege, a feverish disemboweling of sacred precepts. A God is enthroned so cruel as to despise those He created. The wings of beauty are clipped so that this bird of universal truth cannot soar beyond parochial walls. And history, the great teacher of mankind, is transformed into a slave. And this violence against God and beauty and history is done to dehumanize Black people and then to justify their degradation.

Without the Black man, America in the past might have been truly great. With the Black man, the nation's possibilities for human achievement have no limit. But white Americans prefer to coddle the germ of the disease that is atrophying the limbs of Europe. White Americans still blindly insist upon regarding the collective attainments of humankind as snapshots in a racial family album. Under the weight of racism, America, land of many peoples, amalgam of as many cultures, clings to the dangerous myth that it is a "white" country.

Only the black men of Africa, holding wealth and power securely in their grasp, will teach America at long last that her sons of slaves are a key source of her strength, just possibly of her survival. And the black men of Africa will have that wealth and power. That is what I had come to understand at the end of my first day in Guinea. And believing it, I could go home again. I had been freed of a great burden.

As I opened the wooden gate, a watchman guarding the hotel darted out from the unfinished main floor to challenge me. I produced my key and he retreated into the shadows. *"Bon nuit, patron,"* he murmured. Upstairs I lay awake for awhile, listening to the night sounds of Africa, strange and yet familiar. Voices of unknown, unseen animals, and of sleeping men. The sounds seemed never to entirely cease. I fell asleep with the soft chords of the cora caressing my ear.

". . . Above all, we American Negroes should know that the center of the colonial problem is today in Africa; that until Africa is free, the descendants of Africa the world over cannot escape chains. . . ."
—W. E. B. Du Bois, 1946

1970

THE
AFRICAN ACTUALITY:
A PERSONAL JOURNEY

THE REALITY OF AFRICA CAN BE ENOUGH TO drive a Black man to despair, if that man believes that genuine freedom for Black people all over the world will come only when Black Africa holds genuine power. That eventuality, of course, presupposes that unity will have come to that great, sprawling, diverse continent, that African technology will have applied itself to exploiting and controlling the vast natural wealth of the land, and that the last vestiges of colonialist hegemony will have vanished. Africa in the year 1970 stands nowhere near such an eventuality. There is no African country at all where Black men manage more than the mere mechanics of government; everywhere that there is industry and "development" and important commerce, Europeans and Americans are the *de facto* rulers; technology, without which none of the richness in the earth can be mined and transformed into the wealth necessary to educate the people and to modernize the nations, remains a white monopoly, and the greedy white capitalists intend to maintain exclusive possession of technology for as long as they can arrange it. And all the forces of history, logic and human frailty conspire with them to guard their prize.

To begin with, most of Africa suffers in spades the Black American disease of worship-of-whiteness. The roots of the plague, of course, lie in our similar histories. In parts of Africa, the European presence has been an inglorious fact since long before the slave ships brought the first cargo of our ancestors across the Atlantic. From the Cape northward to Ndola to Luanda to Kinshasa to Ibadan to Bamako to Oran, the vision of "the good life" is cast in colors generated out of the civilization of the West. The human and cultural models which have overwhelmed the Africans have all been deeply antagonistic to all that is native to Africa. It is logical, then, that people who have learned contempt for their own life-styles, and subsequently for themselves, should seek a fullness in the alien image. It is perfectly logical, however demeaning and pathetic it also may be, to see a blue-black Wolof steaming in a Cardin suit from Paris on the burning streets of Dakar, a white woman at his side. The man has believed, as he was intended to, that he approximates wholeness as a human being to the degreee that he "evolves" toward the French ideal, and having invested all the physical energies and all the intelligence of a lifetime in eager pursuit of the ideal, he will struggle with that desperation characteristic of the subconsciously doomed against any suggestion that he is a neuter and a fool.

It is a frustrating thing to sit across a table from an *Ivorien* intellectual at a sidewalk Cafe in Paris and have him patronize you, a Black American, because you live in a country where open racism rules your life, by saying to you, with all his imitative Gallic gestures, that life in Abidjan is completely free of similar racism from the French. . . . There is no place to begin. The irony, the anomaly, the simple silliness—they are all too obvious and monstrous to deal with. The man does not see the ridiculousness of his situation. There he sits in France, bedraggled, with neither a penny nor a pot, drinking cognac you have paid for, bragging of the relative liberality of Frenchmen who, in fact, remain in power in his own land a decade after he has gone through the pageantry of "independence," proud that white men no longer assert their social superiority over him in his own country, as if they had a need to.

It is a mind-boggling experience to go to dinner in the penthouse executive suite of a European-owned industrial firm in a newly independent African country whose vital services have been virtually paralyzed by the malicious exodus of European technicians and to have the host, a polished Cheshire cat of a man, grinningly cite the impotence and ignorance for which he and his kind are responsible as proof positive of the inability of Africans to govern themselves.

In Africa, everything is yet to be done. Kinshasa is a bustling city now, full of money and luxuries and employed Congolese, but the Belgians are back in ever-growing numbers, and it is the Belgians who own the factories and direct the commerce. The traitor Moise Tshombe did not succeed in wrestling Katanga from the Congo for his European masters, but the vital industries in that province, as in all the others, belong to Europe. In Zambia, the technicians in the basic copper mining industry are white, some of them South Africans, and Kenneth Kaunda is in the humiliating situation of having to rely on the criminally racist government of Zimbabwe (Rhodesia) for power and transport. In the Ivory Coast in 1970, there are in excess of 60,000 Europeans, six times as many as there were before Felix Houphouet-Boigny took over the government in 1960, and all of them are wealthy compared to the *Ivoriens.*

Kaunda, a proud and cautious man, is trying to tackle the monumental problem of transferring real power to his people. So is Julius Nyerere in Tanzania. And Sékou Touré in Guinea. They are trying, knowing the formidable odds against them, knowing that they can suffer the fate of Kwame Nkrumah whose vision for Ghana and for all of Africa posed a threat to vital European and American economic interests. They know. And with what resources they have, and can muster, they are moving forward, watchfully. The dangers are very great, but the stakes are no less than the future of Black men everywhere.

In South Africa, and across the whole southern sector of the continent which contains some of the loveliest land and much of the continental wealth, white men are in repressive control of the lives and destiny of millions of Black people. It is a scandal and an intolerable affront to Black men everywhere that this should be so. Somewhere in the back rooms, in the secret chambers of their minds and ministries, Black seekers of power should be plotting the downfall of the white regimes in Zimbabwe, in Namibia (Southwest Africa), in Angola, in Mobambique, in South Africa and in all the little enclaves white men maintain in strategic corners of the continent.

Black Americans need to understand their relationship to Africa, but they need, at the same time, to understand the forces which stand between them and the dignity of which only a free, strong Africa can assure them. To understand this, they must divest themselves of all the romantic

The African Actuality: A Personal Journey

notions about power in general and of the power of Black men in particular. The journey to that understanding might be painful, but it is an educational journey no serious Black American can afford not to take.

* * * *

In January 1959, I gave up the little pink-colored stucco villa in which I had lived for a year on the island of Mallorca and took a French boat across the Mediterranean, through the Straits of Gibraltar and down the African coast to Guinea. Four months earlier, Sékou Touré had said *"Non"* to Charles DeGaulle, rebuffed the idea of a permanent union with France, and set the mineral-rich little West African territory on the road to national independence. That the act was necessary and inevitable cannot be questioned by anyone who believes in freedom and self-determination for all peoples; that the act was courageous can only be appreciated by those who have a knowledge of Guinea—or of any other African colonial territory—prior to political independence.

Naturally, in Guinea, as in most colonial territories, little effort had been spent on training Africans in such important technical skills as operating telecommunications systems, building and maintaining roads, managing factories, controlling electrical and water processing plants, piloting airplanes—or even conducting the routine business of a post office. These tasks had been customarily assigned to Europeans. And the French colonialists, enraged at Touré's audacity in rejecting them, had performed an act of incredibly petty vindictiveness: they had withdrawn in great haste, cancelling many crucial services for the populace, crippling others, and leaving vital lines of communication and key functions in conditions of chaos. What *l'independance* meant for Guinea had very little to do with romantic notions of sudden wealth and power for a formerly subject people; what it did mean, of course, was that a whole new world of possibility was opened up to the people, provided that they had the energy and the determination to pursue it—and the necessary leadership that would direct them through the countless traps and troubles which lay strewn along the path toward true political and economic independence.

During my stay in Guinea, I met most of the leaders of the country and was befriended, significantly, by French aides to the President who had chosen to remain in the face of implicit objections by their own government in Paris. Most important to me at the time, I was privileged to have several audiences with President Touré himself despite the great demands on his time and the monumental problems he faced in translating the idea of *l'independance!* into social and economic viability. The talks with Sékou Touré proved instructive not only then, for the light they shed on Guinea and its problems and his plans for solving them, but also later, when I read in the international press accounts of Guinea's plight and of Sékou Touré's approach to easing it. Sékou Touré had risen to prominence in Guinea through the labor unions; he had been schooled in Marxism, as he had learned the inner-workings of capitalism, and he clearly saw socialism as the means of developing his country; his strength of mind and personality had served him well in combat with the finest intellects and political leaders in France's labor establishment and even in the French Parliament where he also served, and his love of Africa had endeared him to its people and provided him with the solid base which was essential for his role as national spokesman. In assuming the presidency, Sékou Touré had announced to the world that he had no plan to impose any of the prevailing political ideologies on his people. Yes, he saw some form of socialism as a necessary approach, but that did not mean that he would be subservient to Moscow. Yes, advanced technology would be necessary in mining the huge deposits of bauxite in the country, for instance, but that did not mean that he would invite the industrialists in to take over the national economy. His stance was eminently logical, but the international press, led by the Americans, branded him "Marxist," suggested that he was in the Soviet camp, and proceeded to predict doom for the fledging nation.

One of the people I had encountered during my last days in Guinea was the *Time* magazine representative from South Africa, a middle-aged white American who had brought with him as "cover" an African from Ghana. The white man did not speak French, and his uneasiness in the company of Africans was obvious. He spent much of his time seeking out and communicating with Europeans who remained in the country for one reason or other, usually because of business holdings they were unable to liquidate quickly or profitably. His subsequent report on Guinea and its president in *Time* magazine reflected his incapacities. It was a biased story, hewing to the Touré-is-a-Marxist line and suggesting that Guinea, in rejecting French tutelage, faced dire economic consequences.

The prediction, of course, partially came true. "Of course" because the power of the American government and American industry helped to make it come true. When Charles DeGaulle turned his back on Guinea in an effort to punish the country for opting for independence, France's principal allies—Britain and America—joined her in withholding economic aid from the infant black nation. It will be remembered that it was little Ghana, the neighboring English-speaking nation which had gained independence a year earlier, which came to Guinea's immediate assistance with what aid it could spare. Kwame Nkrumah's gesture also represented a concrete manifestation of his Pan-African Union philosophy, a philosophy which the capitalist nations viewed as an especially urgent threat to their design for Africa.

Only a few months before Guinea became the first African nation under French colonial hegemony to declare itself independent, *Time* magazine had published an elaborate spread on the French African territories, citing Guinea and the Ivory Coast as the two richest of the territories and the two possessing the greatest potential for important industrial development. The Ivory Coast preceeded to play its intended role even after political independence, and it is now one of the key centers for European and American investment in Africa. The number of Europeans in the Ivory Coast since independence in 1960, has increased sharply, most of them holding down technical and managerial jobs in the mushrooming industries, the same positions, in fact, which they held under colonialism. In 1967, even the pro-French president of the Ivory Coast, Felix Houphouet-Boigny, expressed alarm at the rate at which the country's wealth was being exported, some $20 million a year, not including the profits taken out by European firms.

Guinea's development, naturally, proceeded at a much slower pace. Sékou Touré refused absolutely to admit European and American industrialists under their own terms, steadfastly insisting that Guinea hold the controlling interest in any enterprise undertaken in the country under foreign auspicies. When the Guinean government turned East to Moscow, Peking and East Germany for help, the West smirked, "See, we told you so," and hoped for the worst. The worst duly happened. But Sékou Touré only reaffirmed his original position: in later ousting the Russians and the Chinese, in turn, he proved that he would not submit the Guinean people to any ideology which did not suit their special needs and desires. Necessity has forced the Guinean government into certain compromises, but none of them are likely to deter the country from its chosen independent socialist direction. Over the past two years, Guinea has negotiated economic pacts with France and invited European and American firms to exploit the mineral wealth of the nation under very strict regulations designed to leave Guinea in control.

In 1959, several European and American firms already were involved in mining and processing bauxite from the rich fields of Guinea. They had come in under the colonial government, and their franchises had to be renegotiated. Some of them chose not to remain under the black government's terms. The largest of the firms at that time was FRIA, a conglomerate owned by firms in four foreign countries, Olin-Mathiessen representing the United States. FRIA owned a new skyscraper building in Conakry with elegant modern offices and a penthouse apartment and executive suite worthy of a Playboy spread. All of the executives of FRIA were European, but the complex had instituted a program of training Guineans to take over some technical jobs at the mines in the interior. The government made it very clear that Africanization of local industry was one of its aims. Toward that end, a new city was rising around the mines, with industry-built housing for the workers one of its more important features. FRIA was envisioned as a model of cooperation in the industrial development of former colonial territories.

I had gone down to Guinea with some ambiguity of motivation. I had left the United States in 1957 because, quite literally, I no longer could live there. That was the year of Little Rock, the hope-shattering spectacle of a powerful nation writhing willingly, like a sick and pathetic cur, in the throes of a self-induced malignancy. But more than that: daily, across the nation, racists of every conceivable description were demonstrating their utter contempt for Black citizens and for the laws ostensibly designed to protect them. "Law and order" was a charade. The incessant assault upon Black humanity was terrible to bear. What thrust me deepest into despair, however, was not the open defiance of the law and the calculated brutality of the whites, from whom I had never expected very much, but, rather the impotent wailing and apparent apathy of the blacks. I was more than old enough, of course, to know that Black people understood their alternatives—acquiescence or annihilation—but I was also enough of a rebel and self-respecting man to be unable to play the game of survival on the accepted terms. It was difficult then, just as it is difficult now, not to label black people as "cowards" for adjusting to the humiliations which they face as a matter of course in America. But, well, there always is the other side of that coin, the strength of love and wisdom which enabled the race to endure, the great power and beauty of the blood against an evil as monstrous as any ever faced by humankind. That knowledge could sustain me with Black people, but I possessed no resource which enabled me to tolerate the racist abuses of whites. So, when one day on the streets of Chicago, I found myself on the mildest of provocation lashing out in physical fury at an arrogant Polack, I knew that my own safety demanded that I put distance between my country and me.

Europe had provided the relief I needed, but that relief, by definition, was limited. I was a Black man, and an American, on the soil of *Europe,* a situation electric with all kinds of contradictions and ironies, the most obvious of which was the fact that I did not belong there, had no genuine roots there. As a student in Detroit, I had associated very closely with a fine old gentleman named Fred Hart Williams, founder of the Azalia Hackley Memorial Collection in the Detroit Public Library and a historian of Blacks in the Michigan-Ontario geographical area. From him I had absorbed a deep interest in Africa, leading to the development of friendships with Africans studying in the Detroit area. The eventual liberation of the African continent, heralded by the independence of Ghana in 1957, had excited me, and I suppose I entertained some notion of one day going there. On the island of Mallorca, where I settled in Europe, ships sailing to Mediterranean ports from the African continent often stopped in Palma, and the occasional sight of Africans strolling the glittering *paseos* in their exotic *boubous* and *agbabas* quickened my longing to go to Africa. When I finally made up my mind to go, the decision was prompted as much by the subconscious recognition of a longing for roots as it was by the rather vague wish to be involved in the great new adventure on the African continent which had such overwhelming significance for Africans everywhere.

Africa, in a very direct way, fulfilled my desire for rootedness. I will never forget the experience of waking one early morning in the harbor of Dakar, of going to the window of my stateroom and of beholding, with a curious shock, the actuality of Africa. There on the docks below gathered dozens of Senegalese, surely among the blackest of all the African peoples, in white and blue *boubous* which seemed to sweep the ground. Most of these men were stevedores or porters or dock hustlers, and yet they moved and behaved with a dignity and an assurance which was devoid of subservience. As quickly as I could, I dressed, cleared customs and debarked, making my way like an excited child through the streets of Dakar. The odor of Africa was pervasive (I have never been able to figure out just what combination of scents produce the odor which seems to hover over the West African coast), spiked here—I was to learn later—by the scent of roasting peanuts. Dakar is, for most practical purposes, architecturally a French city, appropriately dotted with *places* and parks and dissected by boulevards, some of them broad and sweeping, and modern glass-facaded buildings rise in the city's center and, unexpectedly, in some of the outlying areas. Frenchmen were in evidence everywhere, as were Syrians, Lebanese and Mauritanians, the principal groups constituting the merchant class; but what fascinated me most was the sight of all those Black people supremely self-possessed and "at home," relaxed in a way that Black people in Harlem, on Chicago's South Side, or on Atlanta's West Side, can never be relaxed; the Africans were so certain of their identity that even the idea of it never entered their consciousness; they belonged to the land, and the land belonged to them. There were all those fabulous Black women, undulating along the streets, their carriage as regal as princesses, with all that characteristic rear motion. It was not, of course, an entirely new sight: it is still possible on the rural roads of Georgia, or sometimes on the crowded streets of Harlem, to see Black women move with that gloriously natural freedom which declares a feminity and a grace that relegates to ridiculousness the calculated posturing made fashionable by mannequins and adopted by fashion-conscious women everywhere. The Africanness of the people defeated the Europeanness of the city. Entering the gaudy, colorful, noisy, odoriferous

Sandaga Market at the city's hub was like plunging into the ripe heart of Africa. I willed to be one with these people, and emotionally I managed it. I could later admit my alienness and deal with it, but I would not for the moment allow mere facts to create barriers between me and my spiritual homecoming. I had set foot on the myth-shrouded land of my fathers and here all around me milled people with whom I shared a past reaching back as far as man.

During that first day in Dakar, I toured the city, visited the sparkling new legislative center which had been built as headquarters for the French African Community, the sprawling University of Dakar, the elegant Hotel N'Gor perched on the tip of the westernmost bulge of the continent, the airport, and fabled Gorée Island, from which thousands of slaves had been dispatched to the Americas. This Africa, of course, was not a part of the image that the white man's media had brought to us in America, but then, in all candidness, this Africa was also not of the African's doing. These things I knew very well, though I did not wish to dwell on them then. But the white presence in Africa was a fact with which I would have to deal on every level when I considered the possibility of becoming involved in the great adventure of Africa. And the white presence in Africa proved to be as frustrating and as invincible as it had proven to be in America.

I have already described the situation I found in Guinea. The whole country was in a kind of disarray, and uncertainty characterized the activities of just about everyone, from the president of the republic to the ordinary schoolboy. Sékou Touré wrestled with the difficult problems of governing a new and abandoned nation from which all the old colonial props had been suddenly snatched, including most of the cadre of teachers in the public schools. In the penthouse of

Conakry's one skyscraper, the FRIA headquarters building, the French managers pondered their course; the shelves of the department and grocery stores were nearly empty; and even the gem-like little museum overlooking the sea was deserted, many of its rare treasures gone with the *colons,* many others lying untended on the open ground floor of the building. Recognizing the magnitude of his problem, the president had turned to the people, exhorting them to sacrifice even more, to give their all, to make independence work; and the people had responded, turning out in droves on Sunday mornings to clean the streets and to build roads and clinics with their bare hands (and the Western press reported this public response as "forced labor," as further proof that Sékou Touré had transformed Guinea into a totalitarian state in keeping with his Marxist ideology!). Under the circumstances, there was little I could do in the destitute country (although a FRIA executive asked me to take over the job of driving company vehicles to and from the bauxite mines: the unpaved highway between the mines and the city was dotted with trucks and cars smashed by Guinean drivers insufficiently trained in handling the machines). I possessed no skills which the Government urgently needed, and I had no contribution to make to the struggling economy. Often at night, wandering through the strange dark streets, I wondered at the cruel irony of it all. In America, black people boasted that they constituted a $30 billion market, that their combined income totalled more than that of Canada; and yet, practically none of that great sum of money was at the disposal of an emerging African nation which desperately needed it. Worse than that, none of the black businessmen who thought of themselves as capitalists and big wheeler-dealers had ever bothered to seriously investigate the possibilities of long-ranged investment in Africa. How could they? For most of them, it was an article of faith that Africa had nothing to do with them. In the three months that I spent in Guinea in 1959, I saw only two black Americans: one was Alphaeus Hunton, the brilliant scholar and former Howard University professor whose political beliefs had made him a pariah in his own country and who had gone to Ghana to work with W.E.B. Du Bois on the Encyclopedia Africana; and a grocery store owner from Detroit, whose name was Vernon Yarbrough, a remarkable man who had been a follower of Marcus Garvey and who, quite on his own, had set out to explore his fatherland, intent, if possible, on aiding the development of a new nation with the funds he had accumulated through prudent management of his grocery and of his real estate properties on the lower East Side. (Dr. Hunton, incidentally, died early in 1970 in Zambia where he had gone to teach at the fledging university there.)

My first encounter with Africa, then, had been both inspirational and instructive. I could rhapsodize on the beauty of the Soussou women, the elegance of the Wolofs, and marvel at the incredible energy of the people; but the overwhelming fact about Africa was its helplessness, the staggering task to be performed in transforming potential into power, in pushing the people into the modern technological world as a means of true independence and national survival. I returned to Spain, half-heartedly resumed my life there, knowing finally that I would return to America.

It was five years later after I had come home, in 1965, that I decided again to go to Africa, this time under the auspices of a John Hay Whitney fellowship. It had been my plan to return to Guinea, to tour the country, check out its economic problems and progress, and perhaps write about the country and its valiant struggle for survival. Much had happened in Guinea since my visit there, and a great deal of what had happened had soured the Government even further on America and Americans. Unhappily, the suspicion which the Guineans directed at Americans also included Black Americans, for some so-called "soul brothers" had been prominent in the clandestine activities which had successfully undermined African leadership unacceptable to the West. My overtures and inquiries were met with general coldness, or even with silence, and so I elected to visit Senegal again instead. I was in Senegal when the word came, in February 1966, that Kwame Nkrumah, on a mission to the Far East to persuade battling Indo-Chinese brothers against murdering each other for the benefit of the Western vulture, had been deposed as president of the country he had led to independence from the British. Black representatives of the American government, so the reports say, played key roles in plotting Nkrumah's fall. Sékou Touré, in a brotherly gesture and in the spirit of Pan-Africanism, gave Nkrumah refuge in Guinea. I understood perfectly then why Guinea had not rolled out the welcome mat for me.

Senegal was (is) something else. On my first visit to the country, Senegal was one of the territories which made up French West Africa (the other territories were Upper Volta, Niger, the Ivory Coast, Dahomey, Mauritania and the Sudan—the latter now Mali), and Dakar was the administrative capital of that branch of the French African empire. Leopold Senghor, the eloquent poet-statesman who was now president of the republic had been territorial delegate to the French Parliament in Paris. The French were omnipresent and omnipotent, and the bud of nationalism among the Senegalese gave little indication that it might burst into bloom. In fact, it was not easy to discover among the black intellectuals in Dakar in 1959 voices raised against the French presence and French dominance. Senegalese intellectuals glowed with pride at their status as *evolués* and at the French reputation for racial tolerance. They were French Africans, moving with some ease in French society in Dakar and looking to Paris as their cultural and spiritual capital with no less fervor and dedication than the white men whose heritage was installed there. When I returned to Senegal in 1965, the color of the man who occupied the governmental palace had changed—that man was, in fact, Leopold Senghor himself—but the French remained omnipresent and omnipotent although political independence had come to the country in 1960. Nationalism had blossomed briefly, and Senghor—the great patron of freedom and patriarch of *Negritude*—had found it expedient, as a matter of practical politics, to slap good and patriotic brothers in prison. Clamor for black control shook up the lovely little university nestled beside the sea, but those students and professors who agitated learned quickly enough the overriding fact of Senegalese—and Black African—reality: the fuel that powered the machinery of government came from storerooms owned by white men.

Nor had Senegal's rather large Black intellectual community undergone any significant ideological conversion. Most of these astonishingly vital and attractive men and women still thought of themselves as French Africans, and if they never questioned their loyalty to France it was because, in their view of things, the idea of the necessity of choice between the two countries was never conceivably an issue. There was little discernible difference between the Frenchman's attitude toward Senegal and its problems and the attitude of many Senegalese intellectuals toward his country and its problems. One of the most distressing moments I have ever spent in Africa came during a conversation with a black employee of a United Nations agency on the top floor of a building flanking Dakar's impressive *Place de l'Independance.* We were standing on the balcony looking out over the *Place* and at the blue bay beyond the roofs of the buildings which cascaded toward the sea. The Senegalese, who had once lived and worked in Washington, D.C., and who spoke English very well, had described to me his adventures in America and in Europe, showed me photographs of the woman he had met in Italy and married and of their mulatto children, and invited me to visit him at his flower-bedecked villa in the plush residential suburbs. He knew enough of the United States, of course, to know that racism stalked the back alleys of "the good life" there, and his recitation of his blessings also was a kind of gloat.

"Why don't you get a job and settle down here?" he asked me. "I'm sure you would like it." I told him that my life and my work were in America and that, furthermore, I could not live in Dakar. He smiled indulgently. "The pace here is too slow, perhaps. You are too used to rushing about madly the way the Americans do in Washington, New York and Chicago." I said no, no that was not the reason I had to return to America: my reason had to do with people and serious work that had to be done. But the man thought I had my values all twisted. "Look," he said, as if appealing to a child, "you could have a good life here. Look at me, for example. I come to the office at 10, drive home at noon for a good lunch and a *siesta,* then come back to the office at three and stay until five. When I get home, the servants have dinner ready. Afterwards I relax with my family, or we entertain friends or go out for the evening. What is better than that?" For a moment I could not answer, more out of a sense of futility than absence of retort.

But I finally looked straight into his eyes and with some resignation, asked him if, on his drives to and from his villa at the other end of the city, he ever took the route through the *medina*. My point slowly began to bore in on him. The sprawling section which goes by the Arab word for "native quarter" is one of the most miserable slums in the world. One of the routes to the elegant residential community where the Senegalese *bourgeois* live leads through the heart of the teeming *medina*. "There are slums everywhere," the man said at last, shrugging. "I can do nothing about them." That attitude was, of course, the problem. It was typical of the beautifully educated Senegalese intellectuals that they accepted conditions as they were under the apparent assumption that they could not—even if they cared to—do anything to change them. It was an attitude that did not promise to alter the structure or the identity of the institutions which controlled the country.

Senegal, unlike Guinea, is poor in natural resources, and peanuts have for a long time been the territory's principal cash crop. It must be said that President Senghor has, at least, been realistic in his recognition that the industrialization of the country and the diversificaton of its agriculture depends upon the sympathy and cooperation of powers which possess the financial and technological resources he requires. The dilemma confronting him is classic, and he has chosen to attempt its resolution through "moderate" means—which is to say that he has moved off on an economic course labelled "African Socialism" to distinguish it from, say, Soviet Socialism, and to enable him to institute programs designed to raise the living standards of his people without, at the same time, threatening the investments and the profits of his patrons. His course is fraught with far less peril than that of his fellow-president, Felix Houphouet-

Boigny of the Ivory Coast, precisely because the drive toward nationalism has been blunted by the Senegalese intellectuals's traditional close identification with France and by the fact of the country's basic poverty. President Senghor is also aided in political stability—or, more accurately, control—by the fact that Dakar has served for generations as the cultural, commercial and administrative headquarters of the French-speaking world west of the Congo. The very glitter and dynamism of the city tends to deflect the aim of dissidence. The intellectual unhappy with the Senegalese's tentative hold on the wheel which guides the state can take a kind of comfort in the truth that Dakar, the "little Paris of Africa," is the most graceful and cosmopolitan city between the Sahara and the Cape. But, of course, a European city, benefitting primarily the European populace.

What the Senegalese intellectuals suffer from is the Black skin-white mask syndrome so brilliantly delineated by Franz Fanon. Having accepted colonialism and the values and images of the colonizers, they are incapable of acting as free men, as Africans who hold in their hands the fate, first, of their nation and, finally, of their ravaged and debased continent. "In underdeveloped countries, we have seen that no true *bourgeoisie* exists;" Fanon wrote, "there is only a sort of little greedy caste, avid and voracious, with the mind of a huckster, only too glad to accept the dividends that the former colonial power hands out to it. This get-rich-quick middle class shows itself incapable of great ideas or of inventiveness. It remembers what is has read in European textbooks and imperceptibly it becomes not even the replica of Europe, but its caricature. . . . For 95% of the population of underdeveloped countries, independence brings no change. . . . These hands of government are the true traitors of Africa, for they sell their country to the most terrifying of its enemies: stupidity. . . . In fact, the *bourgeoisie* phase in the history of underdeveloped countries is a completely useless phase. When this caste has vanished, devoured by its own contradictions, it will be seen that nothing new has happened since independence was proclaimed, and that everything must be started again from scratch. . . ." The truth of the latter observation was never so evident as in Senegal, where everything remains to be done. At the university, of course, a vanguard of students know this, inevitably, and they are anxious to begin, first by Africanizing their university, by making it relevant to their true situation and to their real needs, and then by taking over the institutions which control the country, transforming or demolishing them if they do not serve the interests of the people. And several times in recent years, the government has cracked down on the students, making some small concessions in the process but leaving the university, for all practical purposes, a bastion of European ideas and outlook fully in the control of Europeans.

My months in Senegal taught me another dreary lesson: that the American black *bourgeoisie* was not merely content to serve out its useless existence emulating white people in America but that now its members had embarked on far more dangerous and demeaning adventures. They were scattered all over Africa—in the Peace Corps, in the various embassies, as agents of international aid organizations, as teachers, consultants, specialists and representatives of American industries—using their black skins as a shield behind which they carried out schemes calculated to keep Africa weak, exploited and dependent. In Dakar, I met several such people who were conscious agents, blacks who wore their rank with an open arrogance, who lived in a kind of splendor they had never known in America, and who reveled in the fact that they were "making it" on the international scene. As far as I could tell, they made no identification with Africa and its enormous problems beyond a patronizing expression of intellectual sympathy. There were, of course, black Americans in Senegal who had the interests of the Africans at heart—Mercer Cook, the ambassador at that time and an old hand at relating with Africans, among them—but there were enough of the others to lead one to the edge of nausea.

One of these days, the full, awful story of the American secret service's role in the First World Festival of Negro Arts at Dakar in 1966 will be told, stripping of honor certain esteemed Black Americans who lent their prestige to the effort to hold to the barest minimum the political impact of that unprecedented event. As it was, the American Society of African Culture's relationship with the CIA was revealed following the Festival, throwing into full relief the role of AMSAC and its white "friends" in planning American participation in the Festival. It was a sorry affair. Of course, I had been associated with AMSAC in the States, and there had been suggestions that the organization's source of income was suspect, but—like many others—I had chosen to trust the "distinguished" Black men at the helm, even when it seemed that many of them only used AMSAC as a fueling stop *en route* to positions in the foreign service. Almost alone, it seemed, I raged against the lack of interest in involving Black Americans in the Festival. In Dakar, under what I later learned was the most calculated of circumstances, I met AMSAC's "friends" in villas by the sea and argued the impropriety of whites presuming to represent Black America at a Festival of Negro Arts. The "friends" of AMSAC told me, pointblank, that Black Americans had never assumed responsibility for providing funds for such

The African Actuality: A Personal Journey

an endeavor and that, had they not taken over, there would have been no Black American representation at all at the Festival. On one occasion, weary at my repeated implications of conspiracy in keeping Black America ignorant of the great Festival, an agent of the American Government (and of the CIA?) finally let his red hair down. *Yes,* he told me, with a sneer that expressed all his racist feelings, *we are keeping Black radicals away from the Africans, and we will succeed. There's a damned good chance that we'll have the French back in control here after a few years!*

I remembered that man's explosion everytime I entered a shop in Dakar or stopped in an airline office or entered a restaurant or a movie or a hotel, for all these places, and others like them, are owned by Frenchmen. His words haunted me everytime I saw Leopold Senghor at a public event, his smiling Norman wife beside him. *Senegal still belongs to France . . . Senegal still belongs to France. . . .*

The American bigot's words were still with me a year later in Paris when, in exasperation, I stalked out of a party, unable to bear the pretensions of a group of vigorous young Senegalese hustlers who found existence in the *demi-monde* of Paris preferable to the life of building a nation at home. It was all of a part, of course. Fanon had said it all.

But there had been other times and other men at Dakar. I remembered spending a quiet evening at the home of a Paris-educated professor, a superior man then out of favor with the Senghor regime. He trusted me enough to include me in a conversation with a colleague, a young man who taught in the local *Ecole Superiere.* These men understood how important it was that Senegal—that Africa—be truly free. They knew that power in Africa would liberate Black men in the Americas and that, together, Black men in Africa and Black men in the Americas could alter the shape of the world. They understood the imperativeness of reaching out across the seas, of following the trail of the diaspora and tightening the bonds which had linked together Black men everywhere.

Between the first time I set foot on African soil in January 1959, and the last time I visited the continent, July 1969, I had learned a great deal about the African reality. That knowledge permitted me to understand the intervening chaos in the Congo, the reactionary pronouncements of Tom Mboya, the choice of economic exploitation of Felix Houphouet-Biogny, and even the fratricide in Nigeria. The wisdom of my African experience made it possible to look back on a Ghana with its natural leader in exile and to comprehend how that could happen. Pan-Africanism, like some of the great men who espoused and preached it— W.E.B. Du Bois, George Padmore, Kwame Nkrumah—was an idea ahead of its time. That people must crawl before they can walk is a truism no less distressing than it is banal. The people of Africa have been crawling. Now they are ready to walk. Pan-Africanism is an idea whose time has come.

That fact is, for me, the central meaning of Algiers 1969. . . . That was what it meant to have Africans from all over the world assembling on the soil of Frantz Fanon's adopted country to consider the direction the peoples of the African continent should take. Houari Boumedienne, host to the First Pan-African Cultural Festival, said that the nature of the problems affecting the African continent, and the choice of solutions to meet those problems, necessitates a maximum of organization and preparation and a high level of consultation and coordination regarding the decisions and the initiative needed to reach a common goal: the final liberation of Africa, the achievement of economic independence and the hastening of development to bring happiness and prosperity to the people of Africa. The singing and dancing in the streets, the pageants and the parades, were more than mere spectacle and entertainment: the festivities were designed to illustrate that for **Africa** (**in** Boumedienne's own words) "culture is a weapon in our struggle for liberation." The idea was manifested in the theme of the Festival symposium, "African Culture: Its Reality, Its Role in the Liberation Struggle, in the Consolidation of African Unity and the Economic and Social Development of Africa."

Algiers was the Black World coming of age. Eldridge Cleaver, in flight from American "justice," had found a refuge in Algiers. Stokely Carmichael, in exile, wore the aura of a maturing statesman, "home" for him now a simple villa in the cool highlands of Guinea. Africa, the Motherland, now opens her arms to her lost children from the slave lands across the seas. In Nigeria, with the cruel and debilitating civil struggle a thing of the past, General Gowon talks about Pan-Africanism. In Zambia, President Kaunda moves to nationalize more of the copper industry. President Nyerere quietly continues the grass-roots efforts towards mobilizing his people's energies and developing the country. The Congo flexes its massive muscles, revealing the logic of Patrice Lumumba's murder and the grand treachery of Moise Tshombe. Africa moves. It is a new beginning. The peril is greater, but there is also new strength and new hope.

ALSO AVAILABLE FROM THIRD WORLD PRESS

Nonfiction

The Destruction Of Black Civilization: Great Issues Of A Race From 4500 B.C. To 2000 A.D.
by Dr. Chancellor Williams $16.95

Black Men: Obsolete, Single, Dangerous?
By Haki R. Madhubuti
Paper $14.95   Cloth $29.95

The Cultural Unity Of Black Africa
by Cheikh Anta Diop $14.95

The Isis Papers: The Keys to the Colors
Dr. Frances Cress Welsing
Paper $14.95   Cloth $29.95

From Plan To Planet Life Studies: The Need For Afrikan Minds And Institutions
by Haki R. Madhubuti $7.95

Enemies: The Clash Of Races
by Haki R. Madhubuti $12.95

Kwanzaa: A Progressive And Uplifting African-American Holiday
by Haki R. Madhubuti $2.50

Harvesting New Generations: The Positive Development Of Black Youth
by Useni Eugene Perkins $12.95

Black Rituals
by Sterling Plumpp $8.95

The Psychopathic Racial Personality And Other Essays
by Dr. Bobby E. Wright $5.95

Black Women, Feminism And Black Liberation: Which Way?
by Vivian V. Gordon $5.95

Fiction, Poetry and Drama

Blacks
by Gwendolyn Brooks
paper $19.95   cloth $36.95

To Disembark
by Gwendolyn Brooks $6.95

The Brass Bed and Other Stories
Pearl Cleage $8.00

I've Been A Woman
by Sonia Sanchez $7.95

My One Good Nerve
by Ruby Dee $8.95

New Plays for the Black Theatre (Anthology)
edited by Woodie King, Jr. $14.95

Earthquakes And Sunrise Missions
by Haki R. Madhubuti $8.95

Killing Memory: Seeking Ancestors
by Haki R. Madhubuti $8.00
(published by Lotus Press)

New Plays For The Black Theatre (Anthology)
Edited by Woodie King, Jr. $14.95

Reconstructing Memory: Black Literary Criticism:
Fred L. Hord $12.95

So Far, So Good
Gil Scott-Heron $8.00

Wings Will Not Be Broken
by Darryl Holmes $8.00

Look for Third World Press titles at your local bookstore or order from Third World Press, 7524 S. Cottage Grove Ave., Chicago, IL 60619. Shipping: Add $2.50 shipping for first book and .50 for each additional book. Mastercard/Visa orders may be placed by calling 1(312) 651-0700.